Caitlin kn[...]**to do. She felt it in her bones.**

He was going to kiss her, and she wanted him to, just as she had wanted to get away from talking about work and dig into his head to try to find those deeper parts she had started glimpsing. She wanted to lean against him so that she could feel his hardness against her and the steady beat of his heart under the palm of her hand pressed against his chest.

This was something that had been simmering under the surface between them for a while.

She had felt it and had ignored it, but it had been there, unlocked because she was no longer just his PA.

The door between them hadn't just opened *for her*. It had opened for him as well, and maybe that was why she hadn't been able to kill the crush she had on him.

Maybe she had *sensed* a spark there waiting to be lit.

Her breathing hitched and she willed him to do what she wanted him to do.

Kiss her.

Cathy Williams can remember reading Harlequin books as a teenager, and now that she is writing them, she remains an avid fan. For her, there is nothing like creating romantic stories and engaging plots, and each and every book is a new adventure. Cathy lives in London, and her three daughters—Charlotte, Olivia and Emma—have always been, and continue to be, the greatest inspirations in her life.

Books by Cathy Williams

Harlequin Presents

Consequences of Their Wedding Charade
Hired by the Forbidden Italian
Bound by a Nine-Month Confession
A Week with the Forbidden Greek
The Housekeeper's Invitation to Italy
The Italian's Innocent Cinderella
Unveiled as the Italian's Bride
Bound by Her Baby Revelation
Emergency Engagement
Snowbound Then Pregnant

Secrets of Billionaires' Secretaries

A Wedding Negotiation with Her Boss
Royally Promoted

Visit the Author Profile page
at Harlequin.com for more titles.

HER BOSS'S PROPOSITION

CATHY WILLIAMS

Harlequin

PRESENTS

Harlequin®
PRESENTS™

Recycling programs
for this product may
not exist in your area.

ISBN-13: 978-1-335-93977-7

Her Boss's Proposition

Copyright © 2025 by Cathy Williams

Harlequin Enterprises ULC
22 Adelaide St. West, 41st Floor
Toronto, Ontario M5H 4E3, Canada
www.Harlequin.com

Printed in Lithuania

MIX
Paper | Supporting
responsible forestry
FSC® C021394

HER BOSS'S
PROPOSITION

CHAPTER ONE

'BEFORE YOU GO…'

Caitlin looked up from where she was busy trying to make sense of her desk, which looked as though a bomb had hit it. There were papers here, there and everywhere; two empty mugs, which she should have taken to the kitchen hours ago; three cute little pots with cuttings that Edith from accounts had given her; and her computer, which was demanding attention. She slammed shut the lid and looked at her boss who had sauntered out of his vast adjoining office and was now lounging indolently by her desk.

He'd caught her by surprise and her heart flipped over. The damned man always had that effect on her, even though she'd been working for him for over two years. He was pure, sinful, alpha-male perfection: six-two, dark hair, deep, dark eyes, lush lashes most women would have killed for and imperious features lovingly honed to perfection.

'Please don't tell me you've got something that needs to be done yesterday, boss.'

'Since when do you refer to me as "boss"?'

'Since I think that you're about to tell me that I've

got to do overtime because something urgent's cropped up. I have to rescue Benji from the sitter.'

'He's a dog. He can wait an extra hour.'

'Angie might have plans.'

'Didn't you once tell me that all her plans revolved around her doggy day-care business? Or has her social life taken off since then? I can't wait to find out.'

Caitlin shot him a frustrated look from under her lashes and began doing something and nothing to sort out her desk because he was making her jittery, standing there and looking at her with lazy amusement.

He had no idea how much he rattled her sometimes because they worked so well together. They were at ease with one another, and so in tune that she could almost predict what jobs he was going to give her and when. Over the time they had worked together, he had given her more and more responsibility and had upped her pay accordingly in a cunning move that made it nearly impossible even to think about quitting.

Not that that thought had once crossed her mind, however much she occasionally railed against the pointless crush she had on him. A crush was a crush was a crush—manageable and, in a weird way, secretly thrilling. Plus, the work was everything she could ever have hoped for—challenging, stimulating, demanding and varied. She listened to friends drone on about how much they hated their jobs and was guiltily aware that it was impossible to join in the chorus.

'Well.' Caitlin gave up. 'What is it you want me to do?'

'Follow me into my office.'

'Should I bring my tablet? What files do I need to access?'

'No files,' Javier threw over his shoulder as he strolled back into his office, leaving her to gape at him with a puzzled frown.

Her boss lived and breathed work. He played hard, and she should know, because she usually ended up making all the candle-lit, romantic dinner-for-two bookings for him, along with all the theatre and opera tickets and expensive gifts of jewellery and perfume.

But, within the walls of his office, all that mattered to him was his work. When he issued a summons, it was always because some new deal had landed on his desk and he needed her to start working on it earlier than yesterday and faster than the speed of light. So what was going on now? She didn't know and not knowing made her uneasy.

She texted Angie about Benji and hurriedly followed him into his office, which was four times the size of hers and equipped with everything from a long, uncomfortable but very expensive sofa against one wall, to a drinks cabinet that housed any and every drink any client could possibly fancy after a long night hammering out a deal. The drinks cabinet was to ensure they were relaxed, he had once told her with a grin, and the uncomfortable sofa was to make sure they didn't outstay their welcome.

Through the bank of glass behind his oversized desk, guests had a bird's eye view of most of London. It was really magnificent. Caitlin never tired of looking down at the city and all the people, tiny and purposeful, scurrying through the streets. From where she had started in life, she'd reached heights she'd never thought she'd ever reach, and she always remembered never to take that for granted. This commanding view of the city from his magnificent office was a daily reminder of how far she'd come.

Right now, Javier had swung behind his desk and was waiting for her to close the door, which she did, before sitting on her usual leather chair slightly to the side. Her hands felt empty, because she was never in here without her trusty laptop or tablet.

'Well?' she ventured into the unnerving silence.

'I have something to discuss with you, Caitlin, that's of a somewhat…personal nature…'

Caitlin stilled. A rush of apprehension washed through her and suddenly she was catapulted through time, away from the happy-go-lucky, twenty-four-year-old woman and straight back to the kid in care who'd always known that discussions of a personal nature were never going to be pleasant. No family had come to adopt her. She'd had to understand that she had come late to foster care and that many people favoured a baby or toddler over an eight-year-old child. Maybe someday soon, she'd hoped, but times had been tough, and many people had found it difficult to make a conscious decision to add an extra mouth to their weekly budget.

She'd had to stop pretending to be Catarina. Her name was Caitlin—plain old Caitlin. There'd been no point getting above herself. And was it true that she'd busily concocted fairy stories about herself? Had told the younger ones that she was just going to be there for a short while because her family was abroad at the moment? She'd known she had to *live in the real world*.

'What's wrong?'

Caitlin surfaced with a jolt from her trip down memory lane, but she had whitened, and her blue eyes were huge as she stared at Javier in silence for a few seconds.

'Nothing,' she muttered.

'You're as white as a sheet. What do you think I'm going to say? Do you think I've brought you in here to sack you?'

'Have you?'

'God, Caitlin, what the hell would give you that impression?'

Caitlin lowered her eyes and clasped her hands on her lap. When she next looked up, it was to find that he had swerved round the desk and was now towering over her with a look of concern on his face. He dragged a chair across and sat down so close to her that she could breathe in whatever aftershave he was wearing.

'I...' She faltered. This man knew nothing about her, not really. No one could have known her better whilst knowing her less. He had no idea that she had been through the care system. Why would he? Why would the personal details of her life interest him? She was a great worker and that was the main thing.

'You look as though you're about to faint.'

'I... I suppose I jumped to the wrong conclusion...' she mumbled in a rushed undertone. 'You know, it's not like you to summon me into your office for anything other than work.'

When she looked into his deep, dark eyes she could

see flecks of amber. Up close and personal like this, she couldn't escape the haughty beauty of his face, the bronzed column of his neck contrasting starkly with the pristine white of his shirt. Nor could she avoid the glimpse of hair on his chest because he had undone the top two buttons of the shirt.

She averted her eyes hurriedly.

'That's true,' Javier admitted. 'But, rest assured, I have no intention of sacking you. No, I asked you in here because…a situation has arisen and I need to know how you feel about taking on…er…some additional responsibilities.'

'I feel fine about that,' Caitlin said promptly, relieved that her darkest fears had been dismissed, although she was curious as to why taking on 'additional responsibilities' required a chat in his office after work hours. Couldn't he just have given her a list of the clients he wanted her to add to her portfolio? She would almost certainly know what to do because she'd been at ground zero with several of them when it had come to putting the basics of several deals in place.

'Who do you want me to take over? If it requires much overtime…'

'These particular responsibilities will undoubtedly require a fair amount of overtime.'

'In that case, I'll have to make arrangements for Benji, and please don't say that he's just a dog. He gets very upset when I'm away from him for too long.'

'He's just a dog.' Javier grinned.

'When I left him for a week four months ago to go on holiday, it took him ages before he forgave me,' Caitlin murmured as she hived off on a tangent. 'Tail between his legs, doleful expression, barely looking at his food...'

'I'd never have guessed, judging from the dog I saw when you made up for lost time by bringing him into work for a fortnight. He seemed perfectly fine, making friends with every single person on the floor, and chewing his way through the Wilson Partners paperwork which you'd left on the table in my office.'

'I could never thank you enough for allowing me to bring him in, Javier.' She meant that as well. Javier could be a stern taskmaster but he could also be oddly thoughtful and empathetic. She thought of the way her tiny little mutt had clamped his teeth into his expensive trousers, and winced. He hadn't uttered a word of complaint. 'I might have to do the same if I have to work overtime here and can't get cover for him.'

'I re-read your CV and saw that you have some basic grasp of Spanish, as well as law and accounting courses you did before you joined me.'

Caitlin frowned at the change of topic. She thought back to her days studying Spanish, loving what she'd learnt at school, finding the language so wonderful and romantic. At the age of fourteen, she'd whiled away many a happy hour daydreaming about being a swooning, Spanish princess with trailing dark locks and soulful dark eyes—as opposed to a plump, blue-eyed blonde with ridiculously untamed hair who'd been placed into foster care because her mother had died from a drugs overdose and who didn't have a clue where her father was, or even *who* he was.

She'd actually thought about going to university to

study Spanish, but in the end hadn't been able to bear the thought of not earning money for years on end. She'd done night courses in basic law and accounting. She'd dabbled in Spanish because it appealed to her whimsical heart.

'I can speak a little,' she told him cautiously. 'My week in Barcelona with Jannah and Ivy was good. I thought I'd forgotten how to speak it, but I picked it up again pretty quickly. I'm not saying I'm going to be able to understand loads of technical stuff, though.'

'You won't have to.'

'What client are we talking about?'

Javier raked his fingers through his hair and shot her a wary look. Accustomed to exerting control over all aspects of his life, he'd lost sleep thinking about the chain of events now awaiting him. A chain of events that had come ahead of schedule, and would be dealt with, but which would certainly change things up considerably in his life.

Strangely, he'd also lost sleep when he'd thought about asking his PA to take on duties that went beyond the call of what comprised her working duty. He appreciated her probably more than she thought, although her frequent huge pay rises should have given her a clue. She was keen, obliging and never balked at taking on extra responsibilities. The last thing he wanted was to put her in a position where she might feel uncomfortable with what would now be asked.

His lack of immediate response instantly made Caitlin suspicious. She narrowed her eyes and looked at him in silence.

'You'll find out soon enough,' he eventually said, glancing at his watch. 'The reason I called you in here is to try and explain what this job will entail before… er…Isabella arrives.'

Again, he felt that sickening lurch as plans made crystallised into shape, form and substance. It was one thing to lay the groundwork but quite another when that groundwork finally came to fruition and he then had to take action. And it made no difference that the action had been considered well in advance.

It also made no difference that this was the right and only course of action in more ways than one. He'd fancied himself in charge of the situation and yet, as he gazed briefly into Caitlin's cornflower-blue eyes, he had the oddest temptation to let go of his control and succumb to a vulnerability he hadn't had since he'd been a kid, wrapped up in the trauma of his mother's premature death. He had a sudden urge to *open up*. Crazy. He was a guy who always relied on his head and never on emotional responses—never. He shut his mind off from memories of a time when he'd seen first hand where raw emotional responses could get a person. He refocused.

'Isabella? What's her surname? I don't remember any Isabellas on your client list.'

'"Client" might not be quite the word I would use to describe her.'

'Javier, this is driving me crazy. What are you trying to say?'

'Isabella is going to be my wife, Caitlin, and your job

will be to show her the ropes here in London, because this will be where we will be living.'

Caitlin's mouth dropped open and she stared at her boss with huge, incredulous eyes. Since when was he engaged to be married? The whereabouts of his last girlfriend might not be known, but what *was* known was the fact that her departure from the scene had only happened a little over a month ago! How fast a worker was he?

'You're *getting married*?'

'I understand that you might be a little surprised...'

'It's none of my business how you conduct your private life, Javier, but your last girlfriend—I forget her name—was around only a matter of weeks ago! An engagement now does seem a little hasty. Unless...'

'Unless?'

'Unless,' Caitlin said quietly, as her heart constricted and her stupid girlish fantasies about her boss began to dissipate like mist on a summer day, 'you were in love with Sylvie and have now decided to rush headlong into a committed relationship in an attempt to recover from a broken heart.'

'I would stay away from trying to analyse my personal life, Caitlin,' Javier said gently. 'But, just for the record, I was far from being in love with Sylvie. Also, I thought you couldn't remember her name?'

'It came back to me.'

Their eyes met and Javier held her stare for a few seconds as he tried to organise his thoughts into something that would make sense to her before Isabella arrived, which she would do in roughly half an hour. He could see her utter bewilderment and was surprised at how much it affected him. He'd become used to her easy-going predictability. Was she shocked, disappointed?

He realised he wanted to see neither of those on her face. Caitlin was by far and away the best PA he had ever had, and that included his previous one—a tough-as-nails battle-axe who had inconsiderately decided to emigrate to Seattle to be closer to her grandchildren. She was attuned to him in ways that he occasionally still found a little startling. Not only was she highly competent at what she did, but she was intuitive. She could pick up the nuances of what people said, and arrive at conclusions about what they thought, which was very handy when it came to reading the direction of many deals that hung in the balance.

Javier lived life in the fast lane and having Caitlin by his side was a blessing he had become accustomed to over the months and years. Not only did he manage his family's vast business concerns, but he also ran his own highly successful hedge fund, and a specialised acquisitions team that sourced promising tech startups and bought them. It paid to have someone who worked to his incredibly high standards and was always willing to put in overtime.

The fact that she was sunny-natured, that she countered his ferocious drive with humour and that she could tease the stress out of him were benefits he was often barely aware of her bringing to the table. Was that why her questioning, puzzled gaze twisted something inside him?

For all that she knew about the superficial aspects of his private life, they kept their respective distance when it came to anything really personal. He knew when she went on holiday, and the broad strokes of what she did at the weekend, but he didn't know what she thought about anything that wasn't to do with work. She'd never mentioned a boyfriend, so he assumed that there wasn't one on the scene, but had there been? Was she looking for love or just interested in furthering her career? Was she even into guys?

She knew who he dated, and when he broke up, but nothing about what he felt about any of those women he dated and broke up with. She certainly would have been caught on the back foot at the revelation that had just been tossed at her. He belatedly thought about what she had said, about his last girlfriend and the fiancée he had now pulled out of the hat.

'This isn't a rebound situation,' he said with discomfort at the intensely personal suggestion coming from someone who had never commented on his life before. 'I've known Isabella since I was a kid. Our families go back a very, very long way, and for some time now it's been a given that we would marry and join our families' two powerful Spanish houses. It works for both of us.'

'She's a childhood sweetheart?'

'I wouldn't exactly put it that way,' Javier admitted. 'At the risk of destroying whatever romantic notions you may have of love and fairy-tale endings, our marriage will primarily be a business deal, and a highly successful one at that. Her family run a prestigious string of international hotels which will slot in nicely with the leisure side of my family's business interests. There are benefits for Isabella, marrying me, and for me there are likewise advantages.' He paused, on the cusp of saying more, but then retreated from the temptation.

That speculative remark about rushing headlong into a committed relationship in an attempt to recover from a broken heart... For the first time, Javier wondered about the deeper places in his PA that he had never glimpsed. Was she into love and marriage? Was there a boyfriend in the background, someone she'd never mentioned? Maybe there was a string of boyfriends. Maybe his PA was a dutiful employee by day and a pole dancer by night.

Dark eyes rested on her for a few seconds, taking in the unruly vanilla-blonde hair, curly, fly-away and currently restrained by a large glittery butterfly clip that wasn't doing the job it was paid to do because escaping tendrils of fair hair framed her heart-shaped face. Her wide, blue eyes somehow managed to look smart and oddly innocent at the same time. She might not be head-turning glamorous, but there was something about her that got under the skin. Was it the fact that she looked as though she was always ready to smile, to laugh, to tease? The impression that there was a whole lot more there than met the eye?

He knew there was. He knew how sharp she was, how expert at reading situations and how fast her brain worked when it came to solving problems. The fact that she revealed little about herself, that she ran deeper than she chose to put on the table, said a lot.

He went for leggy brunettes who were as transparent

as glass: soothing after-work enjoyment, women who didn't challenge him intellectually and who knew from the get-go that he wasn't in it for the long haul.

He lowered his eyes and dismissed suddenly intrusive thoughts about the woman staring at him in silence, the woman with thoughts he wanted to know and who was distracting him from the reason she was in his office in the first place.

He picked up the thread of the conversation. 'Like I said, Isabella speaks reasonable English, but she would benefit from your help in showing her around London in preparation for our wedding. Taking her to various shops…showing her how life works in the city… The fact that you speak Spanish will help matters.'

'You want me to be a tour guide?'

'In a manner of speaking. Arrangements for our marriage have been a little more rushed than might have been expected, so you may also have to pick up the slack on that front as well.'

'Pick up the slack on that front?'

'I've compiled a guest list—close friends and family. At a later date, something bigger will be held in Madrid for business associates in both companies, and all our relatives over there, but for the moment I expect the event to be attended by no more than fifty people.'

'When is all this supposed to happen?' Caitlin asked faintly.

'In a month.'

'A month? That's impossible.'

'There's no such thing as impossible, not when money is no object.'

'Any halfway decent venue might disagree with you on that, Javier. Nice places get booked up sometimes years in advance. Can I ask what the big rush is?'

Javier hesitated, but of course she would be curious, and she had every right to be.

Isabella… That was a story with so many twists and complications, and he knew that he would have to avoid touching upon most of them. Beautiful Isabella, his close friend from childhood, and the secret she carried about her sexuality. He was the only person who knew that she was gay. She'd always been too scared to confide in anyone, despite his encouragement over the years. She was an only child from a deeply traditional family and, like him, she had lost her mother when she'd been young. How could she ever confide her secret to her father? So she'd kept it to herself. And he was free, single and disengaged, playing the field but knowing that he would have to settle down before his thirty-fifth birthday.

An eccentric clause in the family inheritance would only release two beautiful vineyards into his safekeeping if he married as stipulated. Javier wanted those vineyards. He could remember playing there as a child, when his mother had still been alive. He could remember the sound of her laughter and the look in her eyes as she'd stooped and held a fat grape in her hand and told him how it became wine. He longed for those vineyards for the memories far more than for their potential for huge profit.

Years ago, he and Isabella had shaken hands on their marriage of convenience. He would get his wife and she would get the useful cover she felt she needed. They liked each other. What could go wrong? Those were details he would keep to himself. In truth, Isabella's story was not his to share.

Now the time had come, for reasons neither of them had expected, and he needed his PA to fulfil duties way out of her orbit. Isabella was an only child, without a mother figure to navigate this rushed marriage with her. She needed to be here, because this was where she would be living; and, whilst her English was perfectly passable, she needed someone to metaphorically hold her hand while she was in London, at least for a few weeks, until she found her feet. He didn't have the time to devote to hand-holding and he couldn't think of a single woman he knew who could do the job without being a liability in the process.

'Isabella's father has had a major health scare,' he began heavily, and this was certainly the one thing he could tell her. 'Problems with his heart. He's not out of the woods yet. Isabella has been called in to take charge of the entire show in his absence, to make decisions she isn't yet entirely confident making. She's an only child, and of course there are people to guide and advise, but the buck stops with her. Even though she's been geared to head the company, she's not quite there with the experience.

'Aside from that…and whatever her credentials…the business world can sometimes be an unfairly chauvinistic place, and as it stands shareholders are beginning to get the jitters at the thought that things might not be as under control as they would like. At the moment, the word is out that Alfonso is making hearty progress, but alas, that is far from the case, and it'll just be a matter of time before the market responds to the uncertainty and the share prices plummet.'

'Which is where you come in,' Caitlin murmured.

Javier looked at her with appreciation, seeing that she had grasped the situation without him having to explain further, but he did anyway.

'Which is where I come in.' He wondered how he hadn't noticed before just what a good listener she was. Smart as a tack, yes... Talkative, yes... Upbeat in a way he personally found baffling, yes... But, when it came to listening, she was making it strangely easy for him to expand an explanation she hadn't asked for, and made him feel almost regretful about the confidences he had no intention of sharing.

'Like I said, this union between us has taken shape over a number of years. We've both been free to do our own thing, knowing that our destinies would eventually be entwined. It's something...eh...something that suits us both in equal measure. Lots of reasons, but let's just say that it's not only because it might be desirable to merge our powerful interests.

'The fact is that our grandfathers go way back. They were two friends who founded their own fledgling companies with the unspoken agreement that they would always be there for one another—blood brothers, so to speak. An antiquated concept in this day and age, I guess, but a powerful one back then, and that's something that's run true through the generations. There was an occasion decades ago when my family's empire ran into huge problems, and Isabella's family stuck to their word and bailed us out. Now the time has come for the favour to be repaid, hence a wedding a little earlier than either of us had predicted. We marry, and I will steady the ship until things settle into place. It's nothing that hadn't already been on the cards, although it's now been accelerated.'

'It all sounds very…sensible.'

'Excellent description.'

'But what about love?'

'What about it?'

'Don't either of you want…believe…?'

Javier made a sweeping gesture with his hand and smiled crookedly. 'We have an understanding. So, moving on, you'll naturally be compensated for taking on these additional responsibilities.'

'Wouldn't your…er…fiancée rather *you* took on the job of showing her around and making sure she settles in okay and finds her feet?'

'Of course, I'll do the best I can, but I have three deals on the go, so my time is going to be limited, and I think she'll quite enjoy having another woman with her. I'll be honest, there are quite a few things on the list I can't say I'll be that interested in doing.'

'Really? Such as?'

'Shopping for wedding paraphernalia… Sorting out the venue, the food, the décor…'

'Right…pretty much everything, if I'm reading this correctly?'

'You'll have to take some time off work during the day to attend to certain things, I imagine, so I've made sure to get Tricia Bell on standby to cover for you.'

'As long as I have a job to return to,' Caitlin returned lightly.

But she didn't look away when he raised his eyebrows and said with genuine sincerity, 'No one can replace you, Caitlin. She'll be on loan and then routines will be re-established as soon as the wedding is out of the way.'

He tapped into his phone and pushed it across to her. 'I have in mind financial compensation along these lines. Let me know what you think. No need to say anything now, because Isabella will be here momentarily. Go away and think about the package and then we can talk tomorrow.'

His phone buzzed, then he spoke rapidly in Spanish and vaulted to his feet.

'Stay here.' He looked at her as she half-rose to her feet. 'I'm going to get Isabella to meet you.' He smiled. 'Don't be apprehensive. I know this is a little out of the ordinary, but look on it as something of an unexpected break from routine. One that will be financially very rewarding for you. Isabella is a lovely woman. You'll like her.'

Caitlin watched him vanish through the door and remained where she was in a state of numb shock.

What had just happened? Had she just hallucinated this whole bizarre episode? Her boss was getting married, as cool as a cucumber as the world order collapsed around her. Was she due to blink and wake up any time soon?

No such luck. She dialled Angie about Benji and told her to hang on to him overnight, if she could, because she wasn't sure when she could collect him—emergency at work, blah, blah, blah…

Her mind was reeling from a series of revelations she certainly hadn't expected. Her boss…married in a month? A fiancée she'd never known existed? A union sealed with consent from both of them over the years? Had she suddenly been transported to a parallel universe?

No. The bottom line was that she just didn't know her boss half as well as she thought she had because she'd always assumed that he was predictable when it came to women. They came and they went. She booked restaurants and theatre tickets, and then bought elaborate bouquets of flowers when their time was up. None lasted. She'd never thought anything of it, and had happily and guiltily nurtured her secret crush on the guy who was unattainable—the player who would never settle down.

But he was settling down now, and had always planned to settle down with a woman who made sense in his life—a woman chosen from his part of the world, with the sort of wealth and power that matched his. An aristocrat of Spanish descent just like Javier.

Suddenly her innocent crush felt like a mortifying lack of judgement. What on earth had she been playing at? Had she subconsciously thought that there could be something between them, once he'd finally grown bored with his revolving door of gorgeous catwalk models?

She was twenty-four years old; it was time to grow up and get past the one disastrous relationship she had had three years ago. Time to forget the trust she had placed in a guy who had cheated on her with not just one girl, but four, and counting. He had made big promises in the hope of getting her into bed, and she had believed that he was so strong and so devoted, to have resisted the temptation to push her into sex. In fact, there had been no need for him to do anything of the sort, because he had had his needs met behind her back.

Why had he bothered to stay with her? Because he'd wanted to see what it would feel like to sleep with a virgin? Because she'd done all his coursework for him on one of the courses they'd been doing together? Because she'd been useful, adoring, convenient and happy to do all his boring chores when asked, from ironing his shirts to keeping his cat when he was on holiday with his buddies?

She'd so longed for the safety of a committed relationship after a life in care that she had pinned her hopes on a guy who had been the last thing from *safe*. She'd broken up with Andy and had filled the vacancy with a guy who *had* been safe because she could never have him: her beautiful boss. Who was about to be married.

It hurt, and she was angry with herself for hurting, and angry for not quite knowing why it hurt like it did when it was nothing but a harmless crush. Maybe it was the thought of getting back into the dating scene—a place she had never really been to, if she was honest with herself. She had lots of friends and did things in groups. Andy had been a juvenile mistake, but it had reminded her that fairy tales weren't for people like her—girls who had taken hard knocks in their lives and had had to wake up to harsh reality when they'd still been kids. She could dream, and dream she did, but she was pragmatic enough to know the difference between dreams and real life. Real life was waiting out there for her and, in the meantime, dreams were all about her boss.

Lost in her thoughts, musing on her stupid crush and wondering whether there was some rogue gene in her that inclined her towards pointless fantasising, she was only aware of Javier returning when she heard the soft whisper of the outside door being pushed open.

She half-rose as he entered the office with his hand gently propelling a tall, elegant woman ahead of him. Caitlin's mouth dropped open and she managed to make it to her feet with her hand outstretched, even though she was gaping. Her wildly colourful summer dress didn't make her feel cheerful and filled with the joys of a balmy June evening. It made her feel like a cheap, tacky toy from a charity shop. She self-consciously tugged it down as the tall brunette walked towards her with a broad, friendly smile, hand reaching out to take hers.

Isabella… There wasn't a woman on earth who could have looked better with Javier than the one standing in front of her. The models he dated were all stunning, but the woman now reaching out a hand to her was exceptional. Not only was she beautiful but her proud, finely chiselled features were stamped with that veneer of the aristocrat. She was as bronzed as Javier, her eyes as dark as his, and her hair was cropped short, framing a face that could easily withstand the severity of the cut.

Introductions were made and Caitlin heard herself mutter the usual pleasantries.

They really cared about one another. It was there in the softness in his eyes when he looked at his bride-to-be, and in the smiling trust on her face when she gazed back at him.

Caitlin felt the pang of jealousy and swallowed hard. *This* was who Javier de Sanchez was destined to marry: someone as stunning, as elevated socially, as *Spanish* as he was. The last fragments of her idiotic, escapist crush fell away and she forced a smile back at Isabella.

She was probably in her late twenties, perhaps early thirties, and Javier had been right—she was an easy woman to like. Her smile was warm and genuine, reaching her eyes. The hug she gave her now was spontaneous and generous.

'Javier has told me much about you.'

'All good, I hope!' Caitlin exclaimed.

'Of course! You speak some Spanish?'

'I can struggle by at a push.' She smiled as Isabella leant down and pulled her into a conspiratorial, girlish huddle.

'Is good, because this man of mine is not interested in the shopping, and there will be a lot of that to do, I am thinking.'

Caitlin glanced at Javier and shrivelled inside just a little bit more at the warm indulgence on his face.

Isabella began listing off the various things that they could do together: finding flowers for the wedding; a venue; the food. Her brow had knitted, as though she'd been trying to think of what else could be added to the tally… She said the invitations were all in such a hurry because of…

At this point she faltered and looked to Javier for support, then relaxed when he said something very fast in

Spanish, the tail-end of which Caitlin managed to grasp, which was that he'd explained about her father.

'Will he be able to attend the...er...big day?' she asked politely. 'Your father?'

He wouldn't. It was regrettable but, however, needs must. He insisted on the marriage going ahead without his attendance. There would be some relatives there holding the fort, and of course there would be a big event in due course when he was back on his feet.

In the meantime, Isabella was here to acclimatise to life in London, and would travel back to Madrid every weekend to visit her father.

Caitlin could tell that, however much Javier had told her that this was a business arrangement, a marriage of convenience, it was also a love match. She could see it in their easy familiarity and in the way they looked at one another. The thought of arranging their wedding made her insides knot and she ventured to ask whether a professional might not do a better job.

'Out of the question,' Javier told her as he rested his hand gently on Isabella's back, urging her to the door with Caitlin trailing behind them. He glanced over his shoulder. 'I want the personal touch.'

'As do I,' Isabella agreed, glancing back with a shy smile.

'I trust you,' Javier told Caitlin, pausing at the door so that both women could brush past him. 'I know you'll do a good job, but it's more than that.'

He paused and Caitlin tried to stamp out the flutter of crazy, utterly inappropriate *awareness* that swept through her as their eyes met. With her silly crush truly dead and buried, surely there was no room for physical awareness of the guy?

'Oh, yes?' she just about managed.

'Isabella knows no one in London, do you, Isabella? So we're both hoping that you're more than someone who's around for a few weeks to help with the wedding. We're both hoping that you might become…a friend.'

CHAPTER TWO

CAITLIN HAD NEVER thought that friendship could come with such big downsides, and the biggest downside was the fact that, after two weeks, she could say with hand on heart that she really liked Isabella. Not only was she beautiful and smart, but there was a kindness there that Caitlin would never have expected, given the other woman's elevated status.

Shouldn't stunningly gorgeous women born with silver spoons in their mouths be horrible and snobby? Shouldn't they enjoy giving orders and lording it up over the riff-raff? Or had she succumbed to stereotyping? Maybe it was time to change her reading habits.

She'd spent precious little time in the office, just a handful of hours over the previous fortnight, because she had been out and about with Isabella, visiting various venues which seemed magically to have space when the fee they would get fell squarely in the 'eye-wateringly generous' category.

They'd been to florists. Then, just because it was such a nice day, and because Isabella had wanted to see more of London than just do stuff to do with the wedding, they had gone to Kew Gardens. They had strolled around, chatting in Spanish and English, laughing and correcting one another, and had had lunch there with the sun on their faces surrounded by people enjoying a day out just like them.

In the evenings, Isabella duly returned to her fiancé, and Caitlin returned to her small, rented apartment in West London where she caught up on work. The fact that she and Javier's fiancée got along so well, the fact that the guy was going to be married and that he had found love whether he chose to admit it or not, should have completely put paid to all inappropriate attraction. But, much to Caitlin's frustration, her body still continued to do its own thing.

She no longer saw him daily for hours at a stretch, but she still found herself treacherously looking forward to those snatched times when she came into the office to catch up with some of her work. He would walk in and her heart would do what it always did and skip a few beats; her pulses would race and her mouth would go dry. She kept it all to herself. She made sure to plaster a smile on her face when she told him about some of the things she and Isabella had done. Of course, Isabella would be confiding in him as well, sharing news of where they'd been and what they'd achieved in terms of progressing the wedding arrangements, but he asked and she replied. She hadn't talked to him at all of certain concerns she had about the whole wedding scenario because it wasn't her business.

Right now, Isabella was back in Madrid for four days, and she was back in the office and pleased to be back in the routine. Tricia could only handle so much, and there was tons to do. She was busy writing up a report when Javier strode into the office and paused in front of her desk.

Caitlin looked up, eyes travelling along faded black jeans and the black V-necked tee-shirt that clung lovingly to his muscular abs. He had a casual jacket looped over one shoulder.

'You're not in your work clothes,' she remarked.

'Shocking, isn't it? I decided to take the afternoon off to see two of those venues you and Isabella narrowed down on the list of possibilities.'

'Oh.'

'One more to see before the day is out. I intend to make a decision by the end of the evening.'

'Oh.'

'Are we going to get more than just a monosyllabic reply to all my statements?'

But he was grinning, his dark eyes lazy, amused and doing all sorts of unwelcome things to her nervous system. This was an expression she had seen before, one that feathered along her spine and made her shiver. Did he even know that the way he sometimes looked at her—lazy, intense, dark eyes lingering for a second too long—always put thoughts in her head and kept her fantasies alive? Her lips thinned at her own weakness in reading signs that weren't there.

'But Isabella isn't in the country.' She frowned.

'Duly noted.'

'You'll decide without her input?'

Javier shrugged, his expression shuttered as he looked

at her. 'I don't think she'll mind whatever I choose. I am, after all, a fifty-percent shareholder in this arrangement.'

Which, said like that, brought back those concerns that had been wafting around in Caitlin's head for the past two weeks since she and Isabella had begun putting the wedding plans into effect. She hesitated, tempted to say something, but instead held her tongue and looked at him in silence.

'About to say something?'

'Which of the two have you narrowed down?'

He pulled out a couple of creased brochures that had been stuffed in the back pocket of his jeans and held them out to her.

'Good choices,' she murmured approvingly. 'Out of the four, these would have been my top picks, and I think Isabella would have agreed with me. And with you, of course. It's good that you're on the same page.'

She paused and mentally reminded herself that having any kind of physical response to her engaged boss was one hundred percent taboo. 'Because it shows that you think alike, which is so important in a healthy relationship.'

'Thank you for that observation. And out of the two?'

'I don't think that's for me to say,' Caitlin told him politely.

'Nonsense. You must have an opinion. You always have opinions. At any rate, you can share it with me, because I want you to come with me to the next venue. A little female input would be welcome.'

'Javier, this is the sort of thing you should be doing with Isabella.'

'Who is currently in Madrid, so that's something of a non-starter.'

'Can't you wait until she gets back?'

'The sooner the place is booked, the better. Time marches on. Come along; it's Friday, and that work can wait until Monday. I'm sure Tricia can help out on whatever needs doing, anyway.'

'I thought that would involve shepherding your fiancée around and acting as translator when necessary. I didn't think I would be taking on the role of dedicated wedding planner.'

But he was already moving towards the door, expecting her to spring into action and follow him. The thought of looking at a wedding venue with her boss felt scarily intimate. The sight of him in casual clothing, crazily sexy and way too macho for anybody's good, made her pulses leap just a little bit faster as she reluctantly gathered all her bits and followed him out of the office. She was slipping on her cotton cardigan as the lift doors pinged open and he stepped aside to let her slide past him.

'How have you been finding Isabella, and showing her around and introducing her to life in London?'

'She's absolutely charming. I can see why you two are so close.'

'We understand each other, I suppose. As an only child, like me, she's always been geared to taking over the family business, even if many of the nuts and bolts were handled by other trusted CEOs. She studied business and law at university in Spain, and her exposure to outside influences has been less than you'd expect, given her family's high profile.'

Caitlin had been staring fixedly at the brushed matte doors but now she slowly turned to look at him. He was lounging against the back of the lift, although he eased away when the doors opened to the busy foyer.

'She's clearly very smart. She's talked quite a bit about the family business and what's involved, not that I followed every word she said.'

Truly, Caitlin reflected, Isabella and Javier were both so business-like. To her, it seemed crazy that any bride-to-be would be happy to miss something as vital as choosing her wedding venue. But perhaps this was just the necessary ceremony, and the main event would happen when her father was there along with all their relatives in Spain.

As for Caitlin, she had her own daydreams, but in her heart she knew that they were only daydreams. The rich, handsome boss was never going to gaze into her eyes with sudden adoration and get down on one knee. She would meet a nice, ordinary guy one day who would give her the security she needed—the same security she had thought Andy would give her.

Her life wasn't going to be the fairy tales she had spun in her head as a kid. But for Isabella and Javier? They had all the makings of just the sort of grand romance she read about. They weren't two ordinary people leading ordinary lives. They would never have to make prosaic decisions about paying gas bills and mortgage repayments. They were *meant* for the 'swept off feet' thing. And they weren't even bothered about taking advantage of it!

'I did tell you that you would like her.' Javier broke into Caitlin's reverie, snapping her firmly back into the present.

Soon, they were strolling out into the busy, warm summer streets where his driver was waiting for them in a sleek black Range Rover. It was blessedly cool inside from the air-conditioning. Caitlin relaxed back and half-closed her eyes as the car moved smoothly towards the venue they were going to inspect.

She knew where it was, and knew how long it would take to get there, and the answer was 'not very'. Not very long to get to a place she shouldn't be going to because the woman he was going to marry should be the one going there with him. The woman *he loved*. She had seen it shining in both their faces. The memory of that suddenly cut her to the quick and she shot him a fulminating, rebellious look from under her lashes.

'I don't get it,' she said abruptly.

'Don't get what?'

Caitlin felt hot and bothered at this departure from the usual easy-going working relationship they enjoyed. Suddenly, there was an urgency to say what was on her mind. Yes, she was being paid a small fortune to undertake this mission, but still…

She looked at him coolly and seriously. 'I don't feel comfortable making any kind of decision about something as big as a wedding venue on behalf of your fiancée.'

'Since when was I asking you to?'

'Input should come from Isabella. She would care if you chose something she didn't want.'

'I think you're going beyond your brief here, Caitlin. Just a mild word of warning—I didn't pay you for your observations and conclusions about something you don't know about. You say you think looking at a venue with me is out of your scope, but it's a lot less out of your scope than lecturing me on the dynamics of my relationship with Isabella.'

'Point taken.'

'But it's better than you sitting next to me in sullen silence, so go for it.'

'What about the brief I'll be crashing through?'

'If I'm honest, I think I can handle the directness. It's one of the things about you I happen to like.' He smiled and looked at her for a couple of seconds in silence, eyes assessing and amused. 'Even though it's never applied to my personal life. So…spit it out.' He looked away, shielding his expression.

Caitlin drew in a sharp breath and balled her fists because she had a crazy urge to turn him to look at her to see what was in his eyes. Why did he keep doing this to her—making her think that there was an electric charge there, resting untapped just beneath the surface? Was it her yearning for romance getting the better of her, even though she tried hard not to let it?

She breathed in deeply. 'Isabella is just lovely, but she really doesn't seem at all interested in the exciting business of wedding preparations. I understand she doesn't have a mum being enthusiastic behind the scenes, and that this is all rushed, but still…she's a lot more curious about restaurants and things to do in London than she is in hunting down an outfit for the big day, or even picking which caterer she wants for the reception. She hasn't once mentioned a photographer. I talked about having those disposable cameras on the tables for guests to use and she honestly looked at me as though I was nuts.'

Caitlin grinned ruefully at the memory. 'It's as if she doesn't care one way or another whether there are pictures of the ceremony. Who doesn't want a record of the big day?'

Javier shrugged. 'It's going to be a subdued day, a small affair, with her father still in recovery. An elaborate photo shoot would feel a little overblown.'

'It might be subdued but it'll still be significant.' Caitlin thought about all the daydreams she had had about love, marriage and weddings. None of those daydreams resembled what she was helping out with. 'It's not as though you two don't really love one another. If you love someone why wouldn't you want to celebrate properly? I know you say it's all about business, but it's obvious that's barely half the story with you two.'

'Okay, Caitlin. You've now left all goalposts behind, and that's a step too far.'

His voice had cooled and Caitlin felt that coolness like a slap on the face. This wasn't *them*. But then, these circumstances were far from normal. The separation between them had dangerously blurred because she was now involved in his personal life.

Her feelings were compromised. She knew that. The innocent crush was being tested to the limit and it wasn't going away. He had his wife-to-be on the scene, a woman of whom Caitlin was genuinely fond, a woman he clearly loved—and yet she still felt the dangerous pull of attraction when she was with him.

Such as right now. The dark eyes resting on her flushed face did all sorts of wild things to her body she didn't like. Instead of this intrusion of his personal life slamming shut the door between them, it had opened it wide. It had engineered a curiosity inside her and had allowed her imagination to take flight. Right now, she felt faint as she imagined just reaching out and gently touching this guy who was totally off-limits.

She lapsed into tight-lipped, resentful silence.

'You're right,' she muttered eventually as the silence stretched and stretched until she could have heard a pin drop. Thank goodness he had closed the sliding partition so that his driver couldn't eavesdrop on the most awkward conversation on the planet.

She suddenly longed for the easy familiarity to be back, for this edgy tension to melt away. She would put all her intrusive curiosity into a box and return to the cheerful, upfront girl he knew and liked. She knew she could do that. If there was one thing she had learnt in foster care, it was the value of compromise and the wisdom of saying as little as possible that could be held against her at a later date. To survive, she'd had to know how to pretend and toe the line even if, as in this case, toeing the line involved a whole lot of pretence.

They arrived at the venue, which was a glasshouse set alongside a National Trust property. The glasshouse was perfect for drinks and the room inside the beautiful property was perfect for the reception. It was just the right size. Caitlin caught herself imagining the dining area filled with flowers spilling over elegant columns…pink-and-white vintage roses…candlesticks on crisp, white linen tablecloths…the background fading tones of a violinist welcoming the guests…

She abruptly snapped out of the daydream and chatted about the venue, comparing it to the far more modern one, which was the other option.

'And which do you prefer?' Javier asked, when they had both duly looked around.

'Like I said, that's not for me to say.'

'Very restrained for a woman who's never been shy at voicing her opinions.'

'I'm just remembering those goalposts that I accidentally knocked out of my way,' she said truthfully, and he burst out laughing.

'You have a gift when it comes to making me laugh.'

'I suppose that's a compliment?'

Their eyes tangled and now Javier wasn't smiling when he looked at her. She really was something else, wasn't she? Oh, it wasn't as though he hadn't looked at her before. Now, though, with barriers a little askew, looking had a different kind of feel to it, and he shifted to adjust a sudden stiffening of arousal that took him by surprise. This was dangerous territory. This marriage might be a sham but that didn't give a green light for him to start wondering about his PA.

'Of course it is,' he said gruffly. 'You're cheerful and good-natured and smart. Those qualities count for a lot.

And, as far as offering an opinion about a venue goes, it's work of a sort, wouldn't you agree? Goalposts will remain firmly in place. I'm curious as to why you're so tight-lipped about a straightforward question, anyway.'

'Because it's important that you two decide this sort of thing between you, as a couple.' She sighed and he raised his eyebrows, although there was no return of the unwelcoming coldness that had been there before.

'So I'm taking it that you're into the romance of the situation?' he murmured as they climbed back into the car, he giving his driver instructions to Caitlin's flat, which he had the address of on his mobile. 'Red roses and a harpist in the background? Confetti and tossing the bouquet for someone to nab it and join the queue to walk up the aisle?'

'Red roses would be way too obvious, if you really want to know.'

Javier grinned and cast his dark eyes over her, lingering on the fullness of her mouth and the clean, satiny smoothness of her skin. He shifted. 'I'm guessing your parents got hitched in a village church with white petals scattered along the aisle and a horse and carriage to take them away, wherever they got taken away to, for the requisite honeymoon of a lifetime?'

Caitlin looked away. She felt a sudden sting of tears prick behind her eyes and she had to breathe in long and deep to find some self-control from somewhere.

'What's the matter?'

His voice was surprised...soft...urgent...his hand on her arm gentle but insistent. Still looking away, she shrugged, but her eyes were still glazed as he reached to place a finger gently under her chin, urging her to look at him. The touch was soft and brief and it shot through her body like an exploding firework. His dark eyes had gentled and he was staring at her with his head tilted to one side.

He dropped his hand but she could still feel the heat of his finger on her chin, hot and unsettling.

'Nothing's the matter,' she muttered tightly.

'Something's the matter. What is it? What have I said to upset you? You can tell me anything. I hope, after all the time we've worked together, that you know that.'

'I said *nothing's the matter*,' Caitlin told him sharply. 'So please could you just *lay off*? I'm not the only one who can travel past the brief!'

The silence that greeted this outburst was shocking, unheard of. She rushed into instant apology, her words tripping over one another.

Meanwhile, Javier continued to stare at her with undisguised curiosity. Well, well, well… In all the time she'd worked for him, he'd been presented with someone who was cheerful, easy-going and bright. There was depth, for sure, but no dark side. Yet, now, he had seen something in her eyes, heard the sharpness in her voice, and had known that beneath the surface swirled a lot more than he had probably suspected.

Fascinating. It was obvious that she and Isabella had got on like a house on fire, but she disapproved of the way the wedding was being approached, even though he had explained that the situation was simply something that made sense, a business arrangement.

She seemingly disapproved because she was an incurable romantic, yet when he tried to quiz her on that, half-teasing, half-curious, her reaction had been extreme. Why? Was there a story of a broken heart somewhere? She had stronger feelings about his wedding than *he* had, but then he had reason to be jaded by the whole business of love and marriage.

He thought of his father and the way he had been paralysed by his wife's premature death. Javier had understood then, as a young child, that pain and love were interlinked. If someone lost their heart to a person, and the person they loved was then taken away, they couldn't cope. And, when he'd been still a kid, the loss had hurt even more.

Javier shut down that line of thought and returned to the intriguing present. He was suddenly overwhelmed by the urge to find out more about Caitlin.

'I never asked and maybe I should have…' he began softly, lowering his eyes yet alert to every nuance in her.

'Asked me what?'

'About whether all this business with Isabella is getting in the way of your private life. I realise you've had to juggle things around the dog, but is there someone in your life you're also having to juggle things around?'

'Someone in my life?'

'A partner? Boyfriend?'

'No boyfriend.'

Javier glanced at her to see that she was blushing, defiant and challenging, and her lips were tight. His curiosity deepened. When it came to women, he couldn't remember a time he'd ever been curious about any of them. The women he'd dated had been transitory flings. He'd enjoyed them, just as they'd enjoyed him, and getting deep and personal with any of them would have been unthinkable. Even when it came to Isabella, there was no real curiosity, because he knew her so well.

But Caitlin, with her suddenly fluctuating moods, guarded expressions and skittish retreat whenever he seemed to get too close to something she wanted to keep hidden... Well, he was curious now.

'You surprise me,' he murmured, his dark eyes alert to her physicality and absently appreciating what he saw.

'Why?'

'You're young, you have an active social life, you're outgoing and attractive...you should have a queue of men lining up to ask you out.'

'I think you might be living in the past, Javier. These days, women are equally concerned about their careers. Anyway, I've never had a queue of boys lining up to ask me out.'

'Funny. We work so closely together and yet I'm realising that Isabella might know more about you than I do after a couple of weeks.'

'What are you talking about?'

Javier shrugged but he could sense her wariness. 'I think I'll arrange venue number two.'

'Yes.' Caitlin nodded approvingly. 'Since you've made the choice, I'll admit that I prefer it. It's less harsh. Venue one looked expensive, but it also looked quite cold in the brochure, I thought, even though it was beautiful with the high ceilings and the marble columns.'

'Your apartment.'

The driver was slowly pulling up in front of a functional sixties apartment block and Javier watched as she hastily began to unbuckle the seat belt. He'd been here once before, a flying drop-in on the way to the airport to collect a hard copy of a file he'd unexpectedly needed to take with him to New York. He hadn't made it past the communal entrance because she'd met him at the front.

This time, he wanted the tour. 'I'll show you in.'

'There's no need.'

'I wouldn't be a gentleman if I didn't.' He leapt out of the car at the same time as his driver opened her door. Their eyes met and he grinned.

He noted a barely suppressed sigh of resignation and his grin broadened. He was enjoying his PA in a way he hadn't before. He sauntered behind her into the apartment block and up the two flights to her flat, where they were greeted with yelps of barking long before the key was inserted in the door.

'I've never understood why you have a dog. Isn't it more trouble than it's worth, considering you work full-time?'

When Caitlin spun round, it was to find him closer to her than she'd expected and she shuffled a few steps back.

'Angie said she'd drop him back on the way to get some stuff from the pet shop.'

As to why she had Benji... How could he begin to understand her joy at Benji's unconditional love? How could he ever get that, when she'd grown up with nothing to call her own, a dog was something that filled that void and healed her? She spent a good amount of her salary on him and she wouldn't have it any other way.

She was wired. She'd been insanely conscious of him next to her during the entire trip out to see the wedding venue. Why had he insisted she come? She didn't know; she wasn't sure whether it was her imagination, but there had been an atmosphere between them ever since they'd left the office.

And then that shocking outburst! She'd snapped at him for the first time ever and with a sinking heart she'd seen the astonishment on his face.

He was right: he knew very little about her. And now this situation had added a layer of intimacy to their relationship that was unnerving. It made her behave out of character but some gut instinct told her that acting out of character wasn't going to rouse his anger or even his irritation. It was going to rouse his curiosity and she decided that she didn't want her boss to be curious about her. If he started digging, what would he find? He was so astute when it came to reading people and she had a feeling that he could probably give a masterclass in reading women.

How long would it take him to find out that she had a crush on him? The thought of that made Caitlin fidget with embarrassment. She almost wished she'd fabricated a boyfriend to keep any unwanted curiosity at bay, but then wondered what would happen if he asked to meet said figment of her imagination. The tangled web wasn't worth thinking about.

She opened the door, and on cue Benji flew out with frenzied delight, acrobatically leaping into the air and planting his furry body against Javier's legs.

'Benji, stop!' But she was smiling and Javier glanced at her with raised eyebrows.

'Stop!' he growled and the dog instantly pulled back and gazed up at Javier's towering figure with eager eyes, small body vibrating with excitement at an unexpected visitor.

'Thanks for delivering me to my door.'

'May I have a glass of water before I go? Looking at wedding venues is thirsty work.'

He smiled and she stood back as he swept past her into the one-bedroomed flat which she rented. She saw him looking around, glancing at the optimistic posters on the walls of exotic holiday destinations, the bookshelf stuffed with wonderful romantic fiction, the liberal scattering of Benji's toys and the dog basket by the telly in the small living room.

Like having Benji, having a place to call her own was something else she cherished. She couldn't have shared a house even if the rent might have been half what she paid. She'd longed for her own space way too much. It was what came from having a legacy where the only thing that had really been hers and hers alone was her imagination.

He followed her into the kitchen. She poured him a glass of water and watched, standing back, as he swallowed it down, looking at her over the rim of the glass.

She took in the surroundings: the sticky notes on the fridge; the old-fashioned calendar by the little dresser;

the weathered pine table she had bought for a song when she'd first moved in…

He was here…in her flat…eating up the space with his overpowering masculinity… She shivered and felt a tingle of sexual awareness zip through her body like quicksilver. She would have to get a grip. She held out her hand for the glass and gritted her teeth when he shot her a look of knowing amusement.

Benji had calmed down and she reached to pick him up and buried her face against his soft fur.

'That dog has issues,' Javier said, grinning broadly.

'I realise Isabella is in Madrid, so couldn't do the final venue check.' Caitlin ignored his teasing remark, deposited Benji on the ground and continued tersely. 'But…'

'But…?' He scooped Benji up and stroked behind his ear, gazing at her, hip propped against the kitchen counter.

'But next week is wedding dress week,' Caitlin told him flatly. 'You should be around for that.'

'Isn't that supposed to be bad luck? Groom seeing what the bride has in store for him on the big day?'

'It's not about actually *seeing* the dress. I've sourced a couple of places and you could come and collect Isabella when she's finished. It's a special day, and I'm sure Isabella would appreciate the gesture.'

'She said so?'

'Not in so many words, but I've done the maths, and you've been to precisely zero places with her that have anything to do with your upcoming wedding. Surprising her by showing up after the wedding dress appointment would be a nice gesture.'

There was steely determination in her voice. They had it all, she thought bitterly. They were glamorous, aristocratic, wealthy and beautiful. They had the world at their feet. They cared for one another. And, with all those things in place, instead of celebrating the marriage that would unite them for ever they were indifferent and blasé.

While she could only dream of big, white, frothy affairs that belonged to a world she would never inhabit. She didn't even know whether her time would ever come. Would the background she'd never asked for deprive her of a stab at finding true love? Was she destined to have another Andy experience and end up trusting the wrong guy because she was so desperate for security?

Javier lowered Benji back to the ground and watched as, calm now, the small ball of fur padded underneath the table and settled down among the chair legs to peer at them with interest, head resting on his front paws.

'Let me know when and where and I'll try and be there.'

'Aren't you interested at all in what you're going to find when you show up to get married?'

'I'm not really into choosing flowers, and I already know what I'll be wearing: trousers and a shirt. A jacket might be thrown on for good measure.'

'I suppose if the real big event is happening in Madrid later on when Isabella's dad is back on his feet...'

Her voice was strained as she took the conversation back to safer waters.

'Correct. These are just the formalities we're going through, with sufficient icing on the cake so that it passes muster with various friends and business associates.'

Javier knew the complexities of the situation were beyond her. He had filled her in on the barest bones of the marriage he was about to willingly undertake. A marriage that was a little ahead of schedule, although he was thirty-two and knew there was only so long the pair of them could defer the inevitable. He'd known for years that he had a deadline when it came to getting married. The knot would have to be tied by thirty-five for that sliver of his inheritance to pass into his hands, with all its memories and back stories.

He wondered whether he'd expected Caitlin to be as business-like about the job she'd been given now as she'd always been when tasked with doing something that involved his personal life. She'd never made any judgements about the many women who came and went in his life. He'd lazily fallen into the habit of getting her to buy stuff for them—to book outings and send flowers. She'd never once ventured any opinion that he lacked the romantic touch. She'd never once said that it might have been an idea for him personally to have chosen an item of jewellery for whatever woman he happened to be dating at the time instead of routinely delegating the job to his obliging assistant. No wonder he'd lulled himself into thinking that his PA wasn't the romantic soul he now realised she was.

'I should be heading off.' He half-saluted Benji, who instantly sprang to his feet, alert to the possibility of an unexpected run out.

As he headed towards the door, Javier glanced around him one last time. 'Places you want to see?' he asked idly, taking in a couple of the posters she had neatly stuck to the walls in the sitting room.

'Some of them.'

'You have a list?'

He turned to her with a smile and Caitlin looked back at him with a serious expression. She was relieved that he was leaving and yet part of her wanted him to stay because his presence was electrifying. She'd never realised how alive she felt around him until now, when everything was changing and being around him, and feeling that pleasurable tingle, was no longer appropriate.

'I haven't travelled much,' she now confessed, following his eyes to the bold poster of turquoise seas, white sands and a jetty disappearing into deeper blue.

'No school trips? Annual holidays with parents you wanted to swap for friends, because they wanted you home by ten?'

He grinned, moving towards the door, and Caitlin felt that tension again as a past she'd always kept to herself began to nudge its way to the surface.

'Not exactly,' she said vaguely. 'How about you, Javier? Home by ten and bunking down with twelve other classmates on a ski trip in France?' How she'd longed for the normality of that when she'd been a kid, but those trips had been out of reach for her. So she'd had to make do by weaving enjoyable imaginary scenarios in her head about what it might feel like.

'That might have been nice.'

Caitlin paused at the momentary wistfulness in his voice and breached the mental 'don't go there' sign in her head without even thinking.

'What do you mean?'

He had half-opened the door but now stopped and looked down at her thoughtfully.

'A life that's set in stone from birth doesn't allow much freedom of movement,' he murmured. 'As an only child, and heir to a historic family fortune, responsibility was never far away.'

Caitlin knew that at this point she should say something light and teasing, something to release the sudden electric charge, but instead she said, thoughtfully, 'It must have been tough. But still...you would have had some adventures. I know you've travelled extensively.' She smiled wistfully. 'I can't think that having lots of money prevented you from seeing as much of the world as you wanted to.'

'Maybe you have a point, but money can take as much as it gives.'

'What do you mean?'

'I had everything money could buy given in one hand...and in the other, I had childhood normality taken, the small things that money can never buy.'

Her breathing hitched and she blinked at him, not wanting to let go of this moment, but knowing she had to because there was something dangerously intimate going on between them.

She laughed shakily. 'However restricted your life was, Javier,' she breathed huskily, 'I'm betting it wasn't a patch on mine.'

She was riveted by their conversation...by the thoughtful depths in his dark eyes...by the way he was looking at her, a little awkwardly, but with an intensity that was setting her senses on fire.

'Anyway...' She stood back. 'Please don't forget about coming to surprise Isabella after the dress appointment. I'll email you the details. She's such a wonderful woman; it'd be a nice gesture...a nice surprise. It's...it's the sort of...of surprise any woman would really love.' She paused and took a deep breath to get a grip. 'You might be doing a duty, but from what I see you couldn't want a lovelier partner in crime.'

She sidestepped him to open the door and her heart beat like a drum inside her. She only breathed a sigh of relief when the door was shut and she could hear the faint echo of his steps growing fainter as he descended the two flights of stairs to where his driver would be waiting patiently outside.

She needed to get her act together.

As she lay in bed much later, trying to court sleep with thoughts of her boss swooping and swirling in her head, all she could think was...*this feels like losing control...*

CHAPTER THREE

ISABELLA WAS A NO-SHOW.

'I am so sorry, *mi querida*,' she said on the phone, when Caitlin had been at the boutique patiently waiting for twenty minutes, making lively conversation with the young girl with whom the appointment had been made for a personal run-through of what they had.

'What do you mean, you can't come, Isabella?' she asked, half-dismayed and half-irritated. She'd rolled her eyes and smiled grittily at Anna, the twenty-something tasked with helping them.

'Something very important has come up. I am at the airport waiting to board a plane to Madrid. Caitlin, *mi querida*, I would have called earlier but I forget about the wedding appointment until I looked at the calendar on my phone.'

'How could you forget, Isabella?'

Caitlin was genuinely stupefied. Yes, levels of enthusiasm had been running below average when it came to the wedding arrangements, but to *forget* your own *wedding dress appointment*? She had a moment of complete anger, because how often had *she* dreamt of walking down the aisle with a guy who loved her, who wanted to be her husband and take care of her? Isabella and Javier cared deeply for one another, so how could she remove herself to Madrid on such an important day?

'Caitlin, *mi amiga*, I have things on my mind.'

She'd sounded close to tears then and Caitlin reluctantly went into sympathy mode, asked her if her father was all right and if he'd had some kind of relapse. She thought not, because surely Javier would have said something this morning when she had popped in to the office to catch up on her work?

'Have you told Javier?'

'I have to run, Caitlin. I hear my flight being called. I... I have not managed to get through to him. Anyway, he would be working. He probably would not know that today we had to go and see some outfits. You know men, *hermana*—that is not their thing, and for sure not Javier's!'

Caitlin didn't say anything to that because she hadn't mentioned to Isabella that Javier would be coming to collect her post-appointment to take her out for dinner. She'd wanted it to be a surprise for the other woman. What woman wouldn't be tickled pink by that gesture? But maybe she'd just been projecting what *she* would have wanted onto a woman who really wouldn't be that bothered anyway.

'Well.' She ended the call a minute later and turned to Anna with an apologetic expression. 'You heard all that. Isabella, the bride-to-be, isn't going to be coming after all.'

Caitlin looked around the gloriously well-stocked boutique, beautifully laid out on two floors with racks upon racks of froth and lace, and every style of wedding dress any bride-to-be could possibly wish for. The top floor was for fittings, and the dresses there were all designer labels with eye-wateringly expensive price tags. On the ground floor were the less expensive but just as gorgeous dresses, including outfits for mothers of the bride. She could have spent a day there just touching all the lovely lace and silk, and gazing at the veils and tiaras and losing herself in the daydreams she'd had growing up.

'I'm sorry. I think we'll have to make another appointment. Although, at this rate,' she mused, 'I wouldn't be surprised if the excited fiancée doesn't get me to choose something for her to wear. It's just a simple ceremony until the main event later in the year, but even so, something gorgeous in cream silk… A little flared skirt with a matching jacket, perhaps, and some fabulous shoes… I would have even added a hat—just something simple but exquisite, although I'm not sure that's Isabella.'

'Some brides take more of a back seat than others,' Anna said sympathetically. 'Some are just really busy with their careers and simply don't have the time. You'd be surprised at how many last-minute cancellations we get.'

'What a nuisance for you.'

'I have an idea. I mean, you're here now, and I can see how disappointed you are and also…how thrilled you are to be here.'

'Well, it's all so beautiful…'

Anna burst out laughing and winked.

'I'm here on my own before closing and it's not as

though I can sign out early. My boss has eyes in the back of her head. Don't know how she does it. So, as we're both here and I have no client to impress, why don't you be naughty and choose your favourite dress? I can measure you and fit you, just like the real thing. I mean, who knows, you might be back here one day to buy something for yourself! Trust me, I'll make sure you get a healthy discount if you come back for your own dream wedding dress.'

Caitlin's mouth fell open. Suddenly she was Cinderella—a guilty one.

'Wouldn't you get in trouble?' She glanced around just in case 'trouble' happened to be lurking in a corner somewhere.

'My boss would never know that you weren't my client,' Anna said drily. 'And it's not as if I'll be cutting any fabric or sending anything off for alterations. A few pins here and there… No one will know and, if you like, I can even take a picture of you in your perfect dress on your phone, for posterity. Just make sure you don't show your fella!'

'I don't currently have one of those,' Caitlin said absently. She grinned. 'But, if you're *sure*, might be fun. Hey, a girl can dream, can't she?'

For the next forty minutes, the time allotted for the non-appearing fiancée, Caitlin pretended. She was back to being a kid, losing herself in a make-believe world that had always been a lot more fun than the real one; dreaming big dreams she sadly knew would never come true.

She chose a flamboyantly romantic wedding dress,

chattering all the time to Anna, who was as careful and meticulous as if she were the real deal.

Standing on the chair in front of the full-length mirror, Caitlin's eyes were shining as she breathed in the frothy aroma of a wedding aisle lined with flowers… faces turned in her direction…an avuncular vicar smiling and ready to join her in holy matrimony. Somewhere, there would be a little choir of children with their pure voices singing one of her favourite songs, or perhaps violinists. She would have written and memorised a special little speech for her husband-to-be. Someone would be walking her up the aisle—identity to be determined at a later date, but probably one of her girlfriends. And, waiting for her, turning slowly to face her, her dream groom…who looked suspiciously like her tall, dark, handsome boss.

It was a wonderful feeling. She was Cinderella for the very first time in her life and in that moment, everything was forgotten: the sadness of foster care; the eagerness to forge a life of independence; that juvenile broken heart; her improbable crush on her unavailable boss; the topsy-turvy mess of helping to sort out a wedding for a woman she liked to a guy she fancied…

She lowered her eyes, blushing and smiling, and did a little awkward twirl on the chair. When she opened her eyes…there he was: the guy in her wild imagination waiting by the altar for her to sashay towards him.

Javier—her boss.

Except, this wasn't a convenient figment of her imagination. This was *her boss*, standing at the top of the narrow staircase, looking at her in a wedding dress.

Caitlin broke out in an instant cold sweat. Sheer panic combined with paralysing mortification.

She literally couldn't move a muscle as he strolled towards her, his dark eyes resting on her burning face, giving a once-over of the extravagant dress that barely contained her abundant curves—way too many curves for something as elaborate as this. She agonisingly avoided glancing down at her breasts which were bursting out of the snug, heart-shaped bodice.

'Not exactly what I was expecting,' he drawled, coming to a dead stop in front of her.

Caitlin was lost for words. In the heat of the moment, she'd forgotten about Javier; she had somehow assumed that he would be politely waiting outside for Isabella to join him.

He couldn't have looked more devastatingly handsome. He'd come straight from work. His white shirt had been impatiently rolled to the elbows and he'd undone the top two buttons so that she could just about glimpse the dusting of dark hair on his chest.

'I... I...' she spluttered, but before her addled brain could come up with something suitable Anna stepped in front of her and held out her hand.

'I'm Anna.'

'And I'm surprised.' Javier continued to look at Caitlin with amusement. 'Where is my fiancée? Last I knew, you and I weren't engaged to be married, were we?'

He made a show of looking around him for Isabella while Caitlin stood there, desperately wanting the ground to open up and swallow her whole, and not disgorge her until she was very, very far away from her boss.

Anna filled in the blanks. 'Your fiancée unfortunately couldn't make it.'

'So...?' he prompted in a long, lazy drawl.

His eyebrows shot up and Caitlin finally found her voice, although what could she say—that she'd been swept away on a tide of wishful thinking, to the guy who'd probably never crossed paths with wishful thinking and so wouldn't have a clue what she was on about?

'So,' she hedged, 'I thought that...'

'I persuaded her to try on her dream dress,' Anna piped up. 'Good for business.' She winked at Javier, one business person to another. 'If I can get Caitlin to fall in love with a wedding dress from the shop, then I've got a potential customer in the not-too-distant future!'

'I'll get changed,' Caitlin muttered huskily and self-consciously as Anna helped her off the stool and Javier lent a hand, steadying her. She'd gone from feeling on top of the world in her fairy-tale, fantasy wedding dress to feeling like a complete fool.

She burned up as she hurried towards the fitting rooms, having to gather great swathes of fabric as she walked because the dress had been far, far too long for her.

Javier watched Caitlin hurry away, cheeks pink. The petite girl standing next to him was chattering away, obviously trying her best to smooth things over in an awkward situation. He barely heard a word she was saying. This wasn't what he'd been expecting. When Caitlin had told him that it would be a nice gesture to surprise Isabella by showing up post-wedding-dress fitting to take her out for a meal, he'd acquiesced, largely because it hadn't been worth the debate.

He and Isabella communicated daily. She'd chosen to stay at one of his penthouse apartments in Knightsbridge rather than share his house, and he got that. They had an understanding of which Caitlin was unaware. But could he be bothered to argue the toss about whether or not to meet Isabella this evening? No. It had become apparent that his PA was the epitome of romantic. Why disappoint her? She was already utterly confused by his arrangement with Isabella. She'd no doubt been raised on a diet of the traditional fairy stories, where the fair maiden always ended up walking up the aisle to the handsome suitor.

So here he'd come, fully expecting his fiancée to be waiting for him. Instead, he'd rung the doorbell, pushed open the door and headed up the stunted staircase to find… Just thinking about what he'd found made his mind go into instant meltdown.

Of course, he'd noticed those lush curves before, hidden underneath the bouncy but unrevealing work outfits. But to find Caitlin standing on that chair, her face radiant and shining, her body barely contained in a wedding dress that was all pinched-in waist and deep neckline, had been mind-blowing.

'Lush' didn't come close to describing her body. She was the perfect hourglass—slender waist with rounded hips and breasts that were several sizes more than a handful.

He'd felt faint. His libido had duly risen to the occasion and he'd only managed to control his body by focusing on the fact that finding her standing on a chair in full regalia was a shock. He'd kept his eyes fastened to her face, but how could he have missed the push of her breasts against the tight-fitting bodice? There'd been so much cleavage on display that he'd struggled to breathe properly.

And, when she walked off, the sway of those generous hips kept him nailed to the spot, unable to move or even take in what the girl next to him was jabbering about.

Javier didn't do instant lust—not like this. He liked to be in control. Maybe it was because he had been brought up to respect the obligations that came with his family's standing. Maybe a life led on the straight and narrow just didn't allow for anything *but* control. But there were times when he knew that the explanation for the man he was just wasn't so simple.

The loss of his mother had inserted a shard of ice into his soul, and it had only grown as he had matured. Had he ever tried to pull that shard out? Ever tried to see what he could be if he came down from his ivory tower? No. He liked things the way they were because he could never be hurt the way he had been all those years ago, not if he controlled everything and everyone around him. Just as he controlled this marriage, getting just what he wanted from it, and knowing that Isabella was as well, which was a bonus.

He was attracted to women; he dated them, slept with them, got bored and moved on. He had never been so physically bowled over that breathing became difficult but he had been just then.

She emerged in record time, back in the knee-length flowered skirt and the loose green top with buttons down the front. He wondered what it would feel like to undo those buttons one by one and then scoop those magnificent breasts out of whatever bra might be struggling to contain them.

She couldn't meet his eyes, and he had a sudden, primitive urge to tilt her chin so that she had to look at him and tell her that it had been a pleasure seeing her in that dress. He knew that somewhere deep inside she was uncomfortable and embarrassed. Weirdly, so was he. His control had taken a knock.

'Okay,' she said vaguely to no one in particular, before turning to Anna and offering a few stilted remarks about her client who had gone AWOL.

'I'll rearrange,' she said, moving towards him, and yet managing not to catch his eyes.

'I should apologise,' she said, still not looking at him as they made their way down the stairs with Anna following a discreet distance behind to lock up for the evening. She was saying something about being remiss in not making sure the front door was locked while she'd been upstairs. Javier barely heard. He could breathe in the heady floral scent of the woman keeping her distance slightly behind him.

'Apologise for what?'

'I lost track of the time.'

'Apologise for what?' he repeated.

'For... Isabella didn't show up... Well, she called,

actually, to tell me that she had to fly back to Madrid. She didn't say why, so…'

'You're stammering.'

'Can you blame me? I feel uncomfortable about this!'

'I booked a restaurant. Since Isabella isn't here, why don't you join me for dinner?'

'Aren't you bothered that your fiancée has disappeared off to Madrid without telling you?'

'I expect she'll call me later to explain.'

'This is crazy!'

Javier raked his fingers through his hair and paused briefly to look down at her. Her face was pink and angry and he wanted nothing more than to push back her tangled blonde curls and kiss her full, pouting mouth.

'I think your concern is misplaced,' he said softly.

'What do you mean?'

'I live in a different world to the one you're accustomed to.'

'You're not kidding. Don't get me wrong, Javier. I see that maybe you've had an arrangement in place with Isabella for a long time because you're both from the same background, and your families go back a long way, but I don't get why you're both so indifferent about the details when you care about one another. It's not like one of these cases of two people only meeting a week before they tie the knot.'

'Neither of us is romantically inclined.'

'You don't have to have stars in your eyes to want a photographer at your wedding or to show up for an appointment for a wedding outfit with just a week to go before the big day.'

'Modestly sized day.'

'And I'm not having dinner with you, Javier!'

'The table's booked. It would be a shame to waste it. Besides, we can call it a working dinner.'

'What do you mean?'

'Fill in the blanks.'

'What blanks are there to fill in? Hasn't Isabella kept you in the loop about the practical details of what's been booked?'

'Okay, we can fill in other blanks.' He glanced sideways at her and grinned, hailing a black cab and ushering her in before she could protest.

Javier was playing a dangerous game, he knew that, but he couldn't resist the temptation to spend a little longer in her company and find out a bit more about her. His body had betrayed him with a physical reaction that had shaken him to the core and he'd liked how that had felt, danger or no danger. He'd *liked* having a taste of what it felt like to be a little out of control.

What was so wrong with wanting to find out more about her? With this situation in the melting pot, wasn't it natural that he would want to find out a bit more about her? He'd always thought of her as an open book and, now that he'd discovered that she wasn't quite as open as he'd thought, wasn't it only human nature to pursue his curiosity? Wouldn't it actually bring more depth to their working relationship in the future if he knew a little more about her? That seemed a reasonable conclusion and he was happy to stick to it.

'I'm not dressed for a fancy dinner,' Caitlin protested tightly and with impatience.

How had she found herself in the back of a black cab with her boss? She knew. She'd been hot and bothered, seeing him there, staring at her in a damn wedding dress of all things. What on earth had possessed her, twirling around and completely forgetting the time? Had it been sad for her to want to reach out and touch some fairy dust for once? Or had it just been human? Caught on the back foot, she just hadn't been thinking straight. Now she'd followed Javier out and straight into a taxi, her thoughts all over the place.

In between those thoughts of how embarrassed she was, there was also a crazy urge to try and second-guess what had been going on in his head when he'd seen her. Just for a second she thought she'd seen something there, a flare of *something* and, however silly it was to harbour that thought in her head, she couldn't resist pulling it apart and dissecting it.

He was engaged… What on earth was she thinking?

'You're more appropriately dressed than if you'd come out in what you were trying on.'

'Can I ask you to let that go?'

'I'm sorry, it's just that, well, it was quite the surprise.' Javier grinned and, not for the first time, Caitlin wished the ground would open up and swallow her.

Once they arrived at a fabulously Michelin-starred restaurant she could remember having read about a few months back, Caitlin groaned. Could things get any worse?

She glanced down at her work outfit and imagined how much more fitting it would have been for Javier to walk into a place like this with Isabella on his arm. Isabella was like one of those impossibly beautiful heroines she used to read about in teenage romances—the sort she'd pretend to be before returning to planet Earth.

'Hey.'

She raised her blue eyes to his and their gazes locked. Her breath hitched, and she parted her mouth and watched as he automatically looked at her lips before guarding his expression.

'There's no need to be self-conscious,' he told her in a roughened undertone.

'I'm not,' Caitlin returned quickly. She was tense as a bowstring as he reached across to open her door. She had felt the brush of his arm against her breasts, just a brush, and her body had gone crazy in response.

'Sure?'

'I'm just not sure what I'm doing here, aside from filling up a reservation you happened to make.' She sighed. 'I guess we could spend some time talking about work.'

'Or we could leave work chat for another day.'

Typically, with effortless self-assurance, he paid absolutely no attention to any of the looks the other diners gave them. She, on the other hand, couldn't help but wonder whether those curious eyes were trying to work out what a guy like Javier was doing with a girl like her.

When they were seated at one of the tables at the back, he said thoughtfully, 'Isabella has discussed all the things that are already in place. You might not think that I'm that interested—and maybe I'm not as interested as you might expect me to be—but I'm satisfied that you've been efficient in sorting everything out. I realise there wasn't a lot of time, and you've had to do a lot of tricky co-ordinating, and I appreciate that.'

'Thank you.'

'It's nothing less than I would have expected.'

'I'm the consummate professional.' Caitlin grinned reluctantly. 'Plus, I love organising.'

'It's an excellent trait in a PA and, on a personal level, good practice for you—like trying on the dress.' He lowered his eyes, shielding his expression.

'That was stupid and I don't know what you mean.'

'Like the girl said, you're preparing for when it's your turn. I've realised that you're not quite as blasé as I thought you were when it comes to a situation like the one I've thrown you into. When I assigned you to this… project…I had no idea you would find it so difficult.'

'I don't find it difficult.'

'You keep trying to work out why it's not obeying the ground rules you have in place when it comes to relationships.'

'I…' Caitlin opened her mouth to deny that she had ground rules about anything but she knew that that would be a lie. She had tons of ground rules when it came to the sort of lasting commitment that went with marriage.

'You're a hopeless romantic.' He smiled. 'And it's hard for you to understand those of us who aren't.'

'I guess you're right, although not in the way you imagine. I suppose…'

'How so?' Javier was looking at her carefully. 'What do you mean, not in the way I imagine?'

'I mean that, whatever restrictions you grew up with,

you still had advantages most people could never imagine in a lifetime.'

'Like I said, money is not the answer to everything.'

'It's actually the answer to quite a lot, except you wouldn't know about that, because you've never known what it feels like to do without.'

'Is that what you were talking about when you mentioned that your life was as restricted as mine? Tell me about that. Did you grow up with financial hardship?'

Menus were placed in front of them, along with the bottle of wine Javier had ordered, and Javier stared at Caitlin. She fidgeted and lowered her eyes, keen to change the topic.

'So you remembered that.' She flushed.

'When it comes to remembering, elephants and I have a lot in common. Still, I repeat what I said to you, that money comes with its own limitations. Our lives may have been very different from a money point of view but I'm betting we still both had to deal with our own private struggles, big or small. Anyway, when you're young, everything feels big.'

Caitlin was very still as she listened to Javier. Restrictions? She felt tears of self-pity spring up inside her. He might have lived his life in a gilded cage, but she'd lived in a cage as well, and it made a big difference when the bars of the cage weren't made of gold. She thought of the longing she had had for a 'normal' family. She remembered her daydreams, silly make-believe fantasies of things she would never have and places she would never get to go. How *dared* he pry into her life and somehow try and make out that his privileged life had been anything like hers?

'I feel so sorry for you, Javier—prisoner of wealth and privilege with loving parents who only wanted the best for you. So you had your future mapped out,' she said bitterly. 'There are worse things in life than that, believe me.'

'And what are those *worse things* that you're talking about, Caitlin?'

Caitlin's heart hammered. Javier couldn't possibly understand. So, he had had a few despondent moments gazing from his castle at how those carefree kids on the other side of the tracks got on with life. Well, it all felt hopelessly patronising, given her own background. She had done her own gazing, but through the windows of a foster home, just longing to have a family of her own; just to have somebody who really cared whether she did her homework or not. She wished he'd let this go but, like a dog with a bone, he wasn't going to give up asking her questions, and the more she retreated, the further he would delve.

'You really want to know?' Caitlin said shortly.

'I'm all ears.'

'I was raised in foster care.'

The silence stretched and stretched until it became unbearable. For a few seconds, Javier wasn't sure he'd heard correctly. Foster care? It wasn't a revelation he'd expected and, caught on the back foot, he could only stare at her in growing silence.

'You look shocked,' she said defensively.

'I am.' Why bother beating around the bush? He was truly shocked. He'd always prided himself on being able to read people but he hadn't read her. Sudden sympathy flared inside him and he felt as though parts of a jigsaw puzzle had slotted into place, parts he hadn't even realised had been missing in the first place: that curious mix of innocence and robust, streetwise savviness; the apparent openness even though he had always sensed something guarded just beneath the surface, an element of there being more than met the eye.

The image of her in the wedding dress leapt into his head and he drew in a sharp breath. Had that been a lonely child's dream?

'You don't get how Isabella and I could be so casual about something so big as a marriage,' he murmured softly. 'Shall I tell you what *I* don't get?'

'What?'

He waited until oversized plates of food had been set in front of them with flourish, and until more wine had been poured, and then he leant forward and met her wary gaze steadily.

'I don't get how you could be so romantic, be such a believer in love, when you were brought up…in foster care. Didn't you develop a hard shell? Something to protect yourself from the slings and arrows of circumstances you couldn't control?'

'Of course I have. I do believe in love, and I have dreams, but I'm realistic. Because I had a tough childhood doesn't mean it's killed everything inside me. But I look at you and Isabella, with your privileged, cushioned lives behind you—two people who love one another—and I can't believe you would be so casual about your marriage. You treat it as though it's just going to be another day in the week, no big deal.

'Do you know how lucky you are to have found someone who loves you, someone you love back? To have lots of family wishing you well and looking forward to you both tying the knot? So what if there's an element of practicality in getting married? So what? It's still going to be something special, something you should both want photographs of, to look back on down the years.'

She was bright red and her blue eyes were wide and urgent.

Looking at her, Javier had never felt more out of his comfort zone. She looked as though she was about to cry, and he wanted to reach out and rub the tears away before they fell.

She'd put all those dreams she'd woven into a lonely childhood into the idea of some kind of dream, fairy-tale wedding between himself and Isabella. He'd told her that it was a marriage of convenience, but she had translated their mutual affection as some kind of unacknowledged, burning love that was just there waiting to burst free. It was way off target, but oddly incredibly touching.

'I developed a hard shell,' he admitted, thinking back to a background that had been immensely privileged and yet circumscribed. His parents loved him, but it had been a regimented life, and a series of nannies had done most of the graft when it had come to the nuts and bolts of his day-to-day life as a kid.

'To protect you from what?'

Javier said softly, 'To protect me from anything that might have been out of bounds, be that friends from different social circles, hobbies that weren't suitable or risk-taking adventures that were deemed too danger-ous.' He hesitated. 'Fairy tales are built on the concept of falling in love,' he said roughly.

'Yes, they are, and...'

'And that's not the case for Isabella and myself.'

'But...'

'Yes, we care deeply for one another, but we're not in love—neither of us. Caring deeply about someone is all I'm capable of, Caitlin.'

'What do you mean?'

'I lost my mother when I was young,' he confessed, 'and, while foster care may have kept your dreams in-tact against all odds, losing my mother put a torch to mine. When she died my father went off the rails...fell for a younger woman who fleeced him of a fortune. He couldn't handle his grief, and it made me realise that love and loss go hand in hand.' He shot her a crooked smile. 'Affection,' he said, 'is doable, however, and that's what Isabella and I share.'

'Javier, I'm so sorry...'

'We all have our stories to tell,' Javier said drily. He looked at her for a few seconds then said in a quiet voice, 'I think it might be sensible to close the lid on any more personal details, don't you? And one more thing—thank you for sharing a part of your past with me. I wouldn't have pried if I'd known just how private you may have wanted to keep it.'

Their eyes met and he thought, *I've said things here*

that I've never said before to anyone... The lid will def-
initely have to be closed on this because this urge to
confide stops here and now...

CHAPTER FOUR

CAITLIN NODDED SLOWLY at Javier's offer to bring up the drawbridge of privacy between them again. 'That sounds good to me.'

'And,' Javier continued, 'if you feel too uncomfortable dealing with the details of the wedding, then you can devote your time to showing Isabella around London.'

'It's okay, and actually there's not much time to do that, anyway. When she gets back to London, it'll be all systems go until you both get married.' She looked at him thoughtfully. 'And, now that I know a bit more about everything, I'm definitely going to be taking a more practical approach to what's left to be done. I can't imagine how the venue is going to cope with such little notice, but I'll give them a call first thing in the morning.'

'Leave that to me. I am very good when it comes to persuasion.'

'Money can talk,' Caitlin agreed, laughing. She'd ordered an elaborate salad but her mind was only half on the food on her plate as she dug in.

What Javier had told her were confidences, and she could never have foreseen him sharing them in a million years, because he wasn't that sort. Yet he had let her into an intensely private part of his life, and that made her feel…*special*. Their normal working arrangement had shifted and deepened into something more substantial, something that was more personal and more intimate. When Caitlin thought about what he had said about never being able to love anyone because of the loss of his mother, and the collapse of his father in the wake of that, she could feel a swell of tenderness and compassion.

She understood. Experience had a way of carving out which road a person ended up going down. It truly wasn't all about how much money a person had. She'd been blazingly angry when he'd tried to compare the nuisance of living in a gilded cage to the sadness and deprivation of her own foster-care background, but now…

He had suffered his own tragedies and they had scarred him. He had felt the basic structure of his life fall apart when his mother had died, and she couldn't imagine how pitiful it must have been to realise that the one person he should have been able to turn to had removed himself to handle his own grief in a different and destructive way.

Next to her compassion and sympathy, though, was another emotion that wasn't quite as straightforward… He really wasn't in love with his fiancée. Maybe he was truly incapable of dropping his barriers and really *loving* anyone, but this marriage was really one of convenience. She didn't feel quite so bad about the crush that wouldn't budge.

She looked at him from under her lashes, taking in his hard-edged masculinity that she had always found so impenetrable. 'Once you're married,' she ventured into the lengthening silence, 'how is it practically going to work? I know you've just said that we have to close the lid on talking about anything personal, but I'm curious whether you'll still be based here all of the time or not.'

When Javier looked across the table to her, all good intentions of returning to their relationship being strictly business with some light-hearted banter went down the plug hole. He was still shocked at her confession and was seeing her in a new light. He wanted to close his eyes and breathe in deeply when he recalled seeing her on that chair in the wedding dress of her dreams, twirling to some imaginary scenario she'd probably had in her head since she'd been a young girl. At the time, he'd been amused—amused and turned on, because her voluptuous curves were just so unbelievably, unexpectedly sexy.

Now, he wasn't amused. Now, he wanted to take her in his arms, and it was such a crazy feeling that he didn't know what to do with it. He told himself that it was natural to feel sympathy and maybe even a little pity for her story. Life wouldn't have been easy for her. He would probably have felt the same about any one of his employees if he'd found out something about them of that nature. He would have to be a monster not to want to…hold her.

Who was he kidding? If he'd found out the very same thing about Tricia, the bubbly brunette currently covering for Caitlin, he would have been sympathetic enough, produced some tissues from somewhere and given her a bracing pep talk about painful experiences making you stronger. He would never have been tempted to take her in his arms and soothe her back to her usual good-natured self. He would never have gone down the road of saying anything about himself.

Where had that come from?

She'd gathered herself and was looking at him with polite curiosity, which made the logical need to return to normality even less tempting.

'Probably not all the time, at least not to start with. I'll have to be physically present to oversee the technicalities of taking over the business, but I don't anticipate having to relocate there for any period of time. Isabella's family concerns are less significant than my own, bearing in mind I have my own empire that's quite separate from my family's.' Javier was barely aware of their plates being cleared as he looked into her eyes.

Caitlin laughed with genuine amusement. 'When you say stuff like that, I really see what a different world you live in compared to the rest of the human race.'

'There are lots of other people as wealthy as I am.' He was smiling and sat back so that coffee could be put in front of them. His eyes were lazy and amused and sent shivers racing up and down Caitlin's spine.

'But they don't exactly grow on trees.'

'True.' Javier laughed and didn't say anything for a few seconds, although he kept his dark eyes fastened to her face until delicate colour bloomed in her cheeks.

Caitlin licked her lips and sipped some coffee. She felt his eyes on her as she drank and she wondered whether he could see how flustered she was. She hoped not.

She carefully placed the cup on its saucer and kept her eyes lowered for a couple of seconds before looking at him. 'Isabella loves London but she seems quite hesitant about living over here. I hope I'm not out of order telling you this.'

'You're not.' Javier sighed. 'She's going to have to learn to adapt over here, as this is where I'll be based, but that's not to say that she won't be free to come and go as she pleases.'

'Won't you miss her company at all?'

Javier took some time before he answered because the one answer he could have given her that would have been truthful was something that it was not within his remit to do. He and Isabella would discreetly lead their separate lives, respecting one another, while she continued to see the partner she had secretly had for nearly three years.

It was ironic to think that, if she'd had the sort of ordinary background the woman sitting opposite him had probably longed for, she would have had fewer restraints when it came to declaring her sexuality. As it was, her privileged background and the traditional circles in which her family moved had made it hard for her.

He produced the least contentious answer he could think of.

'You know me well, Caitlin. I find work is very successful when it comes to filling in the gaps.'

'And I suppose if you have to flit between Spain and London, you could always time your visits there to co-incide with hers. But what about when a family arrives?' She looked at him thoughtfully over the rim of her cup. 'I'm guessing, even if it's a business arrangement, that you'll both want to have a family?'

'We'll have a family.' Javier looked down, played with the handle of his cup and nodded to the waiter for the bill. 'We both have a responsibility when it comes to that.'

'Well, that'll really mean you'll have to be in one place without too much flitting going on.'

Caitlin looked past him to the ideal family she had always had in her head: four kids, maybe five. She knew that she would have plenty of love to go round. She also knew that she would be there for every one of them, seeing their first steps, hearing their first words, going to the first parents' days... Doing all the things no one had ever done with her.

'That's your background talking,' Javier said gently and Caitlin blinked and looked at him.

'What do you mean?'

The bill had arrived but they were still sitting at the table. Caitlin didn't know about him, but for her there was no one around them. She felt oblivious to every-thing and everyone but for the man looking at her with his head tilted to one side. Was she the only one aware of an electric charge between them?

'Would you like a liqueur?'

'A liqueur? I wouldn't know, because I've never had one.'

'Maybe it's time we remedy that.'

'I really need to go and fetch Benji.'

'Okay.' Javier shrugged and Caitlin immediately decided that Benji could wait a while. Angie was used to her erratic timekeeping. They were friends and they had fallen into a routine of sharing him.

'I mean…'

'Limoncello is very user-friendly.' He beckoned to the waiter and ordered two, but his dark eyes remained pinned to her face.

'Why did you say what you said, Javier?'

'About your background dictating your views on family?'

'Yes, because I don't think my background has anything to do with it. Most people share my views when it comes to bringing up children.'

'Maybe you're right.'

'Why do you sound surprised?'

'Because Isabella and I led a very different life when it came to family bonding. There was bonding but not quite in the way you'd probably understand.'

'What does that mean?'

Javier shrugged. 'What you would expect of most rich dynasties: nannies, help and then even more so after my father's expensive divorce, which brought him to his senses. He never tried to replace my mother again, but he buried himself in work, and I can't say I saw a lot of him over the years. I was, it has to be said, boarding for quite a number of those years.'

'And Isabella… I suppose you'll tell me that her experience mirrored yours?'

'As did quite a few of our mutual friends'. It's a very small world when you live at the very top of it.'

'Can I say something?'

'Why not?' Javier grinned, his seriousness dissipating into amusement. 'I'm not sure I could stop you at this point.'

'I'm guessing that all those women you've dated in the past…' Caitlin sipped the limoncello and winced, although on the second sip it somehow tasted a lot better.

'Go on. I'm eager to hear where you're going with this.'

Javier watched her with brooding intensity, watching the way she delicately sipped the liqueur and the way her eyes flitted to his face and then flitted away just as fast. He'd never had a conversation like this before in his life. His interaction with women tended to be pleasant, fun and superficial. They flirted and he responded and a nice time was had by one and all. He was a generous and considerate lover. He just wasn't a committed one and, when the time came for him to walk away, he could do it without any feelings of guilt because he'd never promised anything. He didn't encourage the sort of deep conversations such as the one he was having here and now.

Actually, he'd never been tempted to. He hadn't thought himself capable of going down that road or even being interested in it. But he was. He couldn't take his eyes off her face and every muscle and sinew in his body was engaged in what she was saying.

'Well?' he prompted.

'I reckon you've gone for a certain type,' Caitlin said

quietly, 'because you've known that you would never be tempted to form an attachment to that particular type.'

'And what type is that?'

'Well…not that I've met them all…but I suppose the type of woman who enjoys being pampered and being seen hanging on to your arm at openings and functions.'

'Tut-tut. Why can't a guy be tempted to form an attachment to a woman like that?'

Caitlin raised her eyebrows but she was smiling because his amusement was infectious.

'Lots of guys can, but my theory is that, even if you and Isabella had never had any kind of arrangement, you would only ever want to settle down with someone like her. Someone from the same social circle you belong to…someone who knows how the ritual of living a life of privilege is handled. And I don't mean a rich life, I mean one that involves tradition and expectation and duty and all that stuff.'

She breathed in sharply and then held her breath, because now that she had said what she'd said she could feel herself hanging on for his answer.

Was she right? Would he only ever seek to settle down with a woman from the same privileged background? It made sense, especially in the light of everything she'd seen and heard. He and Isabella were matched and, if not Isabella, someone like her, someone with the same acceptance of a life of old money and ingrained tradition.

For just a second, Caitlin looked at the place she'd come from and felt like the matchstick girl standing outside in the cold and looking through the windows to where people from a very different world enjoyed a banquet of the finest food. The differences between Javier and someone like her couldn't be more stark, and it was something that had really only crystallised in her head when Isabella had come on the scene.

It didn't matter how he answered her question—of course it didn't!—but she was still hanging on, pretending to smile and be amused while her heart thudded like a drum inside her.

'You're right. I've never given it much thought, but maybe you have a point when you say that I've been having fun with women I never had any intention of settling down with, because I already knew the sort of woman I was always destined to wed.'

Caitlin forced a laugh. 'Understandable.'

'Not that it matters, because I already have my bride waiting in the wings. Which reminds me... I'll be in touch as soon as I hear from her. Everything's in place as far as I can tell so all that's needed now is...'

'Something for the bride to wear.'

'Excellent. Now...' He stood up, glanced at his watch and stepped back, waiting as she followed suit and scrambled to her feet. 'My driver will be waiting outside. I can get him to deliver you back to your house.'

'No need.'

'How did I know you were going to say that?'

He gazed down at her thoughtfully. She was wearing the sort of outfit no woman he had ever dated would have been seen dead in: loose, lots of clashing colour, not even a token nod to a designer. Her hair was all over the place. And yet the pull he felt was intense because he had connected with her on a basis that went far beyond the superficial appeal of how she dressed.

Javier was uneasy with this. He'd never opened up to anyone and he couldn't understand how it was so easy to do so with her. Was it because they weren't involved in any kind of physical relationship? Over the years, Isabella had confided in him, and considered him one of her closest friends, and yet, he realised he had never opened up to her the way he just had to Caitlin.

He had never shared his feelings about his mother and her premature death, and had never voiced how those feelings had changed him for ever. Isabella knew all about his father's lapse of judgement, the way he'd gone off the rails for a while, but had she known anything about how he'd personally *felt* about all that? When Javier thought back to that time, he didn't think so, yet somehow he had shared it with Caitlin. He wasn't guarded with her; that was why. He had always been guarded with women, always watchful for prying questions as a way into trying to seduce him into the sort of relationship he wasn't interested in.

The thoughts were like a low, persistent buzzing in his head as Caitlin hailed a cab, just as his driver eased in front of them and drew to a stop.

'Thank you for inviting me out to dinner, Javier.'

Javier shook his head, frowned and looked down to meet her blue eyes. She gazed steadily back at him.

'Was it as torturous as you'd thought it was going to be?'

'I never thought it was going to be torturous.'

'I had to drag you here kicking and screaming.'

'That's an exaggeration—mildly protesting. I was caught on the back foot because it was a dinner you should have been having with your fiancée.'

'But now you see why the situation may not be quite what you had in mind...'

'We'd said...' Caitlin looked away and took a deep breath before continuing. 'We'd said that we wouldn't do the whole *personal* thing, Javier.'

'So we did.'

'But I just want to say that I have a much clearer picture of your situation and I apologise for falling into the trap of romanticising it.'

As Caitlin ducked into the cab, Javier leant down till he was level with her.

'When it comes to me,' he drawled, 'the best advice I can ever give any woman is to never romanticise about me. I can do flowers and jewellery and tickets to the opera, but romance? That's way beyond my scope and always will be.'

He straightened and stood back just as she turned away so that he missed the expression on her face. He watched as the cab eased its way into the traffic and eventually disappeared left after some traffic lights. He'd enjoyed the evening. Maybe he'd been wrong in assuming that spontaneity wasn't his thing. *Or*, a little voice in his head said slyly, *maybe you've only discovered the joys of spontaneity since your PA has shown a side to her that's got your curiosity going...*

He pushed the voice to one side, preferring not to dwell on that, and began to think about the nature of his arrangement with Isabella. It had all seemed so straightforward when they had talked about it a couple of months previously. They had both recognised that, as only children—both from family dynasties that were bound with ties that stretched from duty into friendship, both with the unspoken agreement that they belonged to family lines that would always protect one another when it came to safeguarding their respective dynasties—marriage was always going to be the desired final destination.

And, as it turned out, one that suited both of them. Within that marriage, they would discreetly lead their own separate lives. There would never be a lack of pleasant companionship and deep affection, and those were powerful bonds that could easily unite two people in a lifelong committed relationship.

As for kids, they would find a way. Medical intervention would achieve the desired result. They cared deeply for one another. There would never be any acrimony between them, wherever their paths led. Whatever their unusual situation, they would make good parents. What could go wrong?

Javier's gut currently told him that there might be more hitches with their well thought-out plan than he might suspect.

He took the car back to his house, resisting the urge to contact her immediately. As soon as he was back at his place, he punched in her number, moving to the kitchen to pour himself a stiff whisky. It was late, but not too late for a nightcap, and he had a sinking feeling that a nightcap was necessary.

Isabella answered on the second ring and he could

tell from the stilted, stressed tone in her voice that whatever she was about to say was probably not going to be
what he wanted to hear.

It was not yet nine in the morning when Caitlin yawned
her way out of sleep and groped towards her phone
which was beeping next to her on the bed. She nudged
Benji aside, eyes half-shut, debating whether to answer
or not, because eight-fifty-three on a Saturday was way
too early for her to take calls. Benji edged his way back
to his original position at her side and resumed snoring.

Which was precisely what Caitlin wanted to do. Her
weekend stretched ahead of her completely empty of
social engagements. It was a blank canvas waiting to
be filled with absolutely nothing in store but pottering,
heading to the nearest park to enjoy the weather and
have an ice cream, and then watching telly in her most
comfy clothes with a bowl of pasta on a tray on her lap
while she caught up on trashy programmes.

Guilty pleasures after an evening that had left her
nerves jumping. She'd felt bonded to her boss in a
way she never had before and suddenly her crush felt
dangerous—something she could no longer write off as
a harmless fantasy. And it was especially dangerous because, even though he wasn't in love with Isabella, he'd
made it abundantly clear he was never going to fall in
love with anyone else…especially not someone like her
who had zero understanding of what it meant to live in
his rarefied world.

She reluctantly took the call and then bolted up-
right when she heard the dark, sexy familiar strains of

Javier's voice at the end of the line. Benji gave a yap of protest and then watched her balefully as she listened to her boss tell her that he needed to have a word with her as soon as possible.

'You're not still in bed, are you?' he asked as an afterthought.

'Of course I'm still in bed!'

'It's nearly nine in the morning.'

'It's also a Saturday. Can I ask what this is about?'

'My driver's on his way to get you, Caitlin. I'd make the journey over to you myself, but I have to take care of a couple of things before I see you, and I can't do that in the back of a car.'

'Your driver is on the way to get me?'

'I'm sorry to have sprung this on you, Caitlin, but... there was no choice. He'll be with you in half an hour.'

'Javier, has it occurred to you that I might have plans for the day?'

'It hadn't, now that you mention it. Have you?'

'No, but...'

'Then that's good news for me. You can bring the dog.'

'Bring the dog where, exactly?'

'My place.'

'Javier...'

'Caitlin, I have to go. I have an incoming call. I'll see you in under an hour and, trust me, if I didn't have to disturb you at the weekend then I wouldn't. I hope you know that.'

She was already hopping out of bed, followed by Benji, whose tail was wagging in keen anticipation of an unexpectedly early start. Javier sounded bright-eyed and bushy-tailed and she knew that he'd probably been up since five. He'd once let slip that he worked out in his basement gym no later than five-thirty as often as he could because by six-thirty he liked to be on the move. That included weekends. She'd privately thought that that must be a big ask for his partners who might prefer someone who didn't leap out of bed at the crack of dawn come rain, hail or shine. But then, not many men could match up to Javier, whether he flung off the bedcovers at five sharp or not.

She showered and dressed at the speed of light and was groggily waiting for his driver at the allotted time. He'd barely given her time to breathe, far less debate what she was going to wear, so she had chucked on a pair of jeans, some plimsolls and a white tee-shirt, with a logo of a famous rock legend, which had shrunk in the wash but was soft and comfortable.

There was no time to take Benji for his morning walk so she packed some food for him and, like it or not, she would have to walk him as soon as she got to Javier's place, whatever urgent situation happened to have arisen.

Still sleepy, she dozed against the car door as she was delivered to Javier's house which, unlike nearly every property in the capital, sat completely within its own grounds with a courtyard at the front that was barely visible behind high black wrought-iron electric gates. The pavement outside was broad and peaceful because all the houses had their own parking spaces behind similarly forbidding gates. Perfectly pruned trees interrupted the pavements, neatly set in equally perfect circular beds. The electric gates eased open and then quietly closed behind them as his driver stopped, killed the engine and then leapt out to open the passenger door for her before she could do it herself.

Benji had been sitting on her lap, tongue lolling out as he eagerly absorbed the passing scenery, and as soon as the car door was opened he leapt out and bolted across the courtyard, tail wagging, sniffing everywhere before leaving his mark on one of the car tyres just as Javier emerged through his front door.

'Sorry,' Caitlin apologised, glancing at Benji before settling her gaze on Javier, who had begun walking towards her. 'But he hasn't had his morning run. I'm afraid he's going to have to run around here till he does what he has to do.' She waved a roll of poo bags at him. 'But I'll clean up, don't worry.'

Her eyes were helplessly drawn to him. Like her, he was in a pair of jeans, but instead of the rock tee-shirt, he was in a loose-fitting white linen shirt that hung outside the waistband. He was wearing very expensive tan loafers. He was the very essence of sophistication and she had to peel her eyes away just to make sure Benji didn't embarrass himself too much on the pristine courtyard.

'Come inside. Have you eaten breakfast? I could get my driver to pick something up from the local deli.'

'I'm fine. I just want to know what's going on.'

It was a wonderful, crazily enormous house with three floors above and one below. It must have been at least ten thousand square foot, with towering vaulted ceilings and a sweeping staircase that travelled upwards in glass-sided spirals so that the magnificent interior downstairs was showcased from every angle. There wasn't a single element to the house that wasn't bespoke.

She'd been here before, in a flying visit to get some stuff for work, and had even joined a couple of clients for a celebration drink post signing a deal, but she still had to be reminded where the nearest downstairs cloakroom was and then how to find her way to the kitchen. Benji was nowhere in evidence and she could only pray that he wasn't discovering the delights of leaving paw prints on white furnishings.

But Javier and Benji were waiting for her as she entered the kitchen and for the first time she noticed that there was a grimness to Javier's expression that she hadn't noticed before.

'What's wrong?' she asked, suddenly very concerned, moving towards him instinctively. 'You're scaring me, Javier. Are you okay?'

'Thanks for the show of concern but I'm okay. I've brought you here because there's been a slight hitch in proceedings.' He'd had his back to her as he fiddled with his coffee machine and now he turned to hand her a cup of coffee, which she took without really noticing, because her eyes were on him.

'What kind of hitch?'

'The wedding is off.'

CHAPTER FIVE

'SORRY. WHAT ARE you talking about?'

'I spoke to Isabella yesterday and, to cut a long story short, the wedding is off. That's why I wanted you here, Caitlin. I didn't think it was a conversation we could skim over in a phone call.'

'How could the wedding be *off*, Javier? We were only planning things out up to a few days ago! I know Isabella has been a little indifferent about proceedings, and I can understand why now that you've explained the situation, but to call the whole thing off? I thought you said that it was an arrangement that suited both of you. Why would she call it off? Are you sure?'

She tried to remember the last time she and the other woman had been out doing wedding stuff. Things had been fine then, hadn't they? As she'd told Javier, the general level of interest might have been well below average, with no noticeable excitement on show, but that was how it had been from day one! She'd become used to it. Had Javier had any kind of hand in this? Could it be anything to do with the heart-to-heart they had had the evening before?

Caitlin looked at him from under her lashes. She

could recall every word he'd said to her in the restaurant, every confidence shared. Had that sharing of thoughts and feelings roused something in him? Had it broken through the hard granite behind which he kept his emotions and freed him to want more than just a business arrangement with a woman with whom he wasn't in love?

'I'm very sure,' Javier said gently. 'It's hard to make a mistake when someone tells you that they no longer want to get married to you.'

'I'm so sorry, Javier. I know that it wasn't a traditional sort of situation…'

'That's a very diplomatic way of putting it.'

'But you must still be disappointed.'

Javier said nothing. He'd known that things weren't proceeding smoothly for the last few days, of course. Isabella had been vague and evasive with him and, when he'd prodded her for an explanation, her eyes had skittered away and she had mumbled something and nothing about everything being fine.

However, that had been far from the truth, as he had found out the evening before when he had called her. Her partner, Maria, who had originally been sympathetic to the situation, had issued an ultimatum. Isabella had realised that to proceed with the marriage would end her relationship with Maria, so she had made her choice.

For Isabella's and Maria's sake, Javier was quietly pleased. The burden of carrying such a big secret would eventually have had consequences. Besides, her fears were unfounded. She might be scared of upsetting the apple cart but how would she ever know if she didn't dive in at the deep end and find out?

Although…the decision did screw with all the plans he had in place. On an immediate level, a deal was in progress for her company that would require a conclusion and, even though he would no longer be involved in the running of her family's business empire, it was only right that he finish what had been started. He had called Caitlin to his house urgently because that was where she would be needed. Not that she had any clue about that.

Then there was the annoying inconvenience of arrangements that had been put in place which would have to be *un*-put. On a much more pressing level, though, was the fact that, with Isabella's withdrawal from the bargain they had agreed, he would now be up against it to find himself a suitable bride before the clock ran out. Isabella had been perfect. Now he was left with a problem. He intended to get those vineyards. When he thought about losing them because of a stupid inheritance clause, he felt sick and his heart tightened up. He wasn't an emotional man, but he had memories of a time of joy and innocence, and he intended to do what it took to have that piece of the puzzle slotted into place in his life.

But he wasn't going to be shackled to anyone who wanted to lay claim to his heart. He couldn't envisage a future of trying not to disappoint a woman who wanted more than he could give.

How many women would fit the bill of the wife who was happy to lead a life of duty without making demands on him? How many women were there out there who weren't romantics at heart, like his PA? How many women would be able to get on board with a marriage that would bring everything they could possibly dream of…except love?

The thought of searching for a suitable bride threatened a headache. He roused himself from his depressing train of thought and considered Caitlin's observation that he would be disappointed.

'Very much so,' he said truthfully. 'Look, Caitlin, I'm sorry if I've sprung this on you,' he said a little awkwardly, 'but as you can imagine there are a number of things in motion that will have to be sorted. Of course, Isabella offered to do that herself, but if I'm honest I think you would be more efficient when it comes to sorting that out.'

'Yes. Of course. Er…can I ask what brought about the change of heart?'

'You can ask, Caitlin, but that wouldn't be a question I would be prepared to answer.' *Or qualified to divulge.*

Caitlin stiffened. When she had been summoned to Javier's house, she hadn't known what to expect. It hadn't crossed her mind that he might have a health issue. She'd never known him to have an hour off work in his life. So she'd immediately thought about some deal or other that was time-pressured and about to collapse. He could be a tough taskmaster when it came to work and would have thought very little of rousing her from her beauty sleep if he needed something urgently.

She'd been knocked for six when he'd told her that the marriage was off. And underneath the shock was just a little thrilling thread of hope that perhaps she'd got to him. Would it have been that impossible? He'd told her things she just knew he would never have told anyone else. She conveniently discarded all the bits of the conversation that didn't tally with the sneaky, treacherous thought that something might have stirred inside him, something that had made him call it quits with Isabella.

That single cool answer to her question brought her right back down to planet Earth and those bits of conversation she had conveniently discarded—the bits that involved a description of the sort of woman he'd seen himself destined to marry had Isabella not been on the scene.

'Understood. I have details of everyone involved in the preparations and all the contact details of the guests. What shall I give as a reason for the cancelled event?'

'No need to give any reasons to anyone. It's off and that's the sum total of it.'

'People will naturally be curious. What if they ask questions?'

'People are entitled to be curious but that doesn't mean their curiosity has to be satisfied. It's a personal situation; maybe you could tactfully imply as such.'

'You're so cool and collected about this,' Caitlin murmured and Javier relaxed enough to half-smile.

'What's the point getting worked up over something that can't be changed?'

'That's true.' The man she'd had dinner with the night before was very different from the guy she was talking to now and she wanted the dinner guy back. She wanted to have that low, sexy voice tell her things he'd never told anyone before. She wanted to feel special and, much as she knew it was wrong and stupid, she wanted to feed the crush that hadn't managed to go away, however hard she'd tried to make it.

She was desperate to see behind the polite mask and the polite words. She *wanted* to play with fire, and that was heady, because she'd never been someone who wanted to do anything dangerous, and this urge felt dangerous.

Andy had messed her around and made her withdraw into a place of guarded caution when it came to her heart. She had trusted what she had seen and hadn't looked deeper at all the stuff that hadn't been visible on the surface. He'd been the safe bet who had pulled the rug from under her feet. She'd turned her attention to her boss because his absolute inaccessibility made him safe, but he was the least safe man on earth when it came to women and their hearts.

He'd said so himself. He'd been honest and straightforward about what he looked for in any woman who might end up occupying a place in his life for longer than ten minutes. Yet the desire to stick her hand out and get it close to the fire was overpowering.

'I knew that growing up in foster care,' she said quietly. Somehow it felt liberating to look back on the past and open up a bit with someone, which was something she'd never done. She looked down and realised that she wasn't doing this to encourage confidences from him, to try and bring some of his walls down. She was doing this because she wanted to.

'Caitlin...'

Caitlin fell silent. When she glanced at him, his dark eyes were urgent, but the second he met her quiet gaze he looked down. The only sign that he had heard what she had said was the tic in his jaw and a certain tension in his body language.

'Talk to me.' Javier's voice was low and ragged and her breathing hitched as their eyes met.

'I'm sorry. This isn't about me.'

'Isn't it? It's not like you're not involved here.'

'What I mean is…'

'I want to hear what you have to say.'

'I guess, when you said that you just had to live with what you couldn't change, it took me back. It was lonely being in care. It's not like anyone was cruel, because no one was. I suppose, looking back, they all gave the best they could, but most of them had families of their own. We were just a job, all of us.'

'I can't imagine what that must have been like for you.'

'Learning to resign yourself to what fate had dealt you was key to surviving intact. I mean…' Caitlin smiled '…I had my fantasy life in my head, but reality, well, that was always a very different thing.'

She looked at Javier thoughtfully. 'So I understand why you're dealing with this calmly. Still, I can't say that I've always been so stoical when it comes to matters of the heart.' She grinned and shot him a teasing look from under her lashes.

'What happened?'

'Oh, the usual: girl meets boy, girl falls for boy and thinks marriage is on the cards, girl finds out boy's been having a bunch of affairs behind her back and only kept her around to help with his coursework. I was upset and it wasn't as though there was anything like a ring on my finger!'

'That's why I find it helps to steer clear of emotional complications, as you know. So, to recap, I'll leave you to make suitable excuses for the non-event but it's all going to have to be done very quickly. At least there are no presents to return to anyone.'

'I'll make sure you approve of the wording before I send anything formal out.'

'No need, Caitlin. You've been working for me long enough and dealing with enough situations out of your remit for me to trust you completely when it comes to matters like this. I'm sure whatever wording you use will be perfect.'

'Okay, if you're sure. On another note, there might be some trouble recovering deposits paid to various people—the venue, for instance, also flowers and the caterer.'

Telling Javier about Andy had opened the door between them even wider for her. As for him, he was still all business, wasn't he? She almost resented the detachment of the conversation they were having, even though to have considered anything else only a few weeks ago would have been unthinkable.

'Pay every single person involved the full amount owed to them as if the wedding had taken place, and add a ten percent bonus to what they would have received from me. They'll have had their noses put out of joint, and it would hardly be fair for them to take the hit with such short notice. Call it a goodwill gesture from me.'

'I'm sure they'll appreciate that.'

'So…moving on to something else.'

'Yes?' Caitlin blinked and dragged her wayward thoughts in line. 'If it's about work, then naturally I can come in first thing on Monday. And… I know you paid me a huge amount to finish this process and now that…'

'Forget about the money.' Javier waved his hand.

'In that case, thank you, Javier. It's been an amazing bonus and it'll help with the deposit I'm getting together.' She paused. 'I'm betting that Tricia will be pleased to get back to her routine. I've been keeping in touch with her, making sure that all the deals on the table when I handed over have been going in the right direction. I can deal with all the stuff with the wedding first thing and be ready to start back by lunchtime.

'Also, if I can bring Benji in, I'm happy to work as much overtime as you need me to. Angie is one of my closest friends, and we pretty much share Benji between us, which he loves, but she refuses to take any money from me for all the cover she provides and I don't want take advantage of her. I'm actually planning to use some of the money you've given me to help her with some building work she needs to house dogs she wants to rescue.'

Javier saw the softening of her features when she talked about her friend and the way she automatically reached down to rub Benji's ears.

For a few seconds, he stared in brooding silence at

her far-away expression, thinking about what she could do to help her friend. She had come from a background of hardship but none of that had dented the soft generosity of her nature. She had no examples of loving parents to have provided guidance with what a successful relationship might look like, but she still believed that they existed. She'd had a learning curve with a partner who had used her, from the sounds of it, and yet she still hoped that she would still find love. She was the essence of the hopeless romantic, whatever hard edges she might have. He felt as though he was looking at someone from a different planet.

'Very laudable.'

She burst out laughing. 'Not really. I'll tell her that she owes me big time.'

Their eyes tangled and she flushed and fidgeted.

'So…is that all? I can start straight away on cancelling stuff.'

She readied herself to leave but Javier held up his hand.

'Not quite.'

'Okay.'

'Isabella and I were due to go to the French Riviera after the wedding for a week…'

'Right. Wow, that's such a shame. I don't remember booking the flights and hotel…' She frowned.

'You didn't. I did it myself. Neither of us was entirely sure how to play that angle and, when we did agree, I handled the arrangements personally.'

'No problem. Add it to the bundle of things to be cancelled and I'll handle it.'

'It's not as simple as that.'

'What do you mean?'

'This was a busman's honeymoon. We discussed what we could combine it with and chose the French Riviera because that's where one of the hotels in her father's chain is being finalised for planning. It was a toss-up between there and Lake Garda. I have a deal nearing completion there, so that would have worked as well.'

'Very…er…practical.'

'Ideally, Isabella would have been there to cast her eye over the architectural drawings—make sure she was one hundred percent satisfied with the finished product, bearing in mind she has a stake in the place—but *c'est la vie*. I've already told Jean Michel, the head guy in place, to supervise everything once work begins and that she won't be coming along with me as anticipated, for unforeseen circumstances. Phoned him before I phoned you, as a matter of fact. Everything's been cleared for me to sign off on the project.'

'Okay, well, that's a result, I guess. If you and Isabella parted company on an amicable basis…um…couldn't she just have gone with you as planned?'

Javier thought of what Isabella was gearing herself up to do—to have the biggest conversation with her father of her life.

'No,' he said flatly. 'But a sense of honour and duty means that I still have to see this deal through.'

'That's so wonderful of you, Javier. I know you two go back for ever, and there's a lot of family history, but many guys would have been tempted to walk away in your situation.'

'I'm not many guys.' He wondered if this was her background kicking in. She dreamt her dreams but her experience with her last partner was probably where her expectations lay when it came to men: hopeful, optimistic, but realistic.

It felt good to think that she didn't include him in that category, which was understandable, considering he was and always had been a pretty fair and generous employer. Nevertheless, he enjoyed the warm approval on her face as she smiled back at him.

'This might have been an arrangement rather than a marriage, in the sense that you understand marriage, but I have and always have had a strong sense of duty.'

It was almost possible to forget the repercussions of the marriage being called off as he basked in her admiring smile. 'But moving on from that...' He reluctantly changed the subject. 'It's not just about the arrangements that have to be cancelled. I called you here because this situation involves you.'

'I beg your pardon?'

'I would have got one of the PAs at Alfonso's head office to join us in France to handle the details of the deal.'

'Alfonso?'

'Isabella's father. He has his own bank of people who could have come into play.'

'Okay...'

'But, with the marriage called off, that no longer seemed appropriate. Still leaves me with the small matter of having someone by my side over there to wrap up the details and format it for signing off. You know the way I work and you can come with me.'

* * *

'Come with you?'

'It's the perfect solution. To be honest, it would have slowed things down having to make sure someone knew how to keep up with me. You know I can sometimes be impatient.'

Caitlin stared at him, mouth open as she digested what he had just said. *She didn't want to go on a work trip with him.* She could smell the danger of that a mile off but he was looking at her with a neutral expression, fully expecting her to comply.

The fact that they had breached the boundary lines between them wouldn't have registered with him. He might have opened up to her, but he wouldn't be dwelling on that, tearing himself apart as he analysed what it might mean. He might have surprised himself but he would not have gone down the road of thinking that it meant anything other than a lapse in his usual rigid self-control, brought about by the suddenly unusual nature of their circumstances.

'I don't think I'll be able to put things on hold without a bit more advance notice,' she ventured and he frowned.

'What would you have to put on hold that requires a lot of notice?'

'I…well, Benji… I've barely seen him recently.'

'I gathered from Isabella that the dog went with you nearly everywhere.'

'Well, be that as it may…and I wouldn't actually say *everywhere*…'

'Do you have an up to date passport?'

'Yes.'

'And no personal obligations that can't be dealt with while you're away for a week?'

'No.' Caitlin sighed.

'Then it's just a matter of packing a case. No need to take care of flights and the hotel is already booked. I'll email you the details.'

'When?'

'A week on Monday morning. Most of the days there will be occupied with work-related issues but you can do your own thing in your spare time.'

'Right.'

'And don't look so worried. I know you've had a hell of a lot sprung on you over the past few weeks, and not much by way of explanation but...' he absently scooped up Benji with one hand, tucked him against his chest and looked at her '...but, once this is out of the way, life will return to normal. Count on it.'

Javier broke eye contact.

Having her there for work was the best outcome but he uneasily remembered how far their working relationship had travelled in the space of just a few weeks. At the back of his mind, there was the unsettling thought that she might have read too much into the confidences he wished he hadn't shared. There had been an intimacy in some of their exchanges; he'd seen her in a different light and had been turned on.

But she hadn't flirted. He was used to women who flirted. If he'd caught the occasional look, well, nothing had been encouraged. In fact, he had made it clear that he was just the sort of guy a girl like her should stay far away from. And she would know that. She knew what he was like first hand from the number of women who had come and gone over time.

He wasn't sure whether asking her on the trip had been the right thing to do but, the sooner their relationship was returned to the box from which it had been temporarily removed, the better. He'd told her that things would return to normal as soon as the deal in France was completed and he'd meant it.

Caitlin didn't feel *normal* as she waited for Javier's driver to collect her on the day of the trip—not unless 'normal' meant jittery, apprehensive and treacherously excited.

There had been no undercurrent of anything when Javier had explained the situation. She would be going there to work. When he'd told her that life would return to normal once that job was done, she'd got the message loud and clear: boundaries, temporarily shifted, were back in place.

She'd packed a compact case with sufficient boring clothes to last her the week. It was going to be hot. She assumed the hotel would have the usual stuff—a pool, a couple of bars, a restaurant or two, and the all-important conference room. So she'd packed one black one-piece swimsuit, a few nondescript work clothes— largely to remind herself that whatever door had been opened between her boss and her would now have to be very firmly shut—and some sundresses, because if she had any free time then she would explore as much as she could.

His car collected her promptly, driver leaping out to carry her case to it, and then holding the door open for her to find that the back seat was empty. She was told that Javier would be meeting them at the airport.

It was a beautiful day and Caitlin relaxed back against the tan leather seat and let her mind drift. She'd never, ever been spoiled by anyone. Care had been practical and regimented in her foster home. She'd always had to pull her weight, help out and then, when she was older, keep an eye out for the younger ones.

Then she'd met Andy, started dating him and had seamlessly moved back into the caring zone, doing stuff for him, and pretty soon he'd accepted that that was her role: to *do stuff for him*. Why should he have lifted a finger when she'd been happy to do all the lifting on his behalf?

Now, as she relaxed in the back of the car, she felt spoiled for the very first time in her life, as much as she tried to tell herself that this was a work trip and nothing more.

Was that how all those women had felt—spoiled and special? Had he made the same effort with Isabella? Or had it been more practical without any need for Javier to go overboard with the courtship?

She gazed off through the window at a cloudless summer day but, although she expected to find them heading towards the congestion of an airport, she realised after a while that they were heading away from London. By the time she'd marshalled her thoughts back to the present, the car was swinging away from the main road and following a winding route to an airfield that was busy with all manner of small planes. Under a milky blue sky, people excitedly hung out behind a sturdy wire fence that was interrupted by gates. Small planes were stationary behind the gates, waiting as one of them taxied its way out into the blue sky to replaced by another.

Javier's private jet was waiting for her, black, sleek and streamlined, and dwarfing all the other tiny single props around it. This was beyond opulence. This was a declaration of untouchability: who owned this beast owned the world. She was aware of eyes curiously following her as she walked towards the jet.

Javier was lounging by the plane, chatting to someone she assumed was the pilot, and she paused, heart hammering, just to stare at him for a few seconds. In cream trousers, a black polo shirt and a cream linen jacket he was utter, masculine perfection. He was wearing dark sunglasses and before she could peel her eyes away he turned to look at her and then sauntered towards her.

'You're here.'

'Mmm. Wow, Javier…is this yours?'

'Everyone needs a toy.'

He grinned as she shielded her eyes from the glare and looked at him.

'It's a very expensive toy.'

'I have a lot of money. Besides, it's very convenient for getting from A to B very quickly, and it's easy to work on board. You could almost say it pays for itself. Did you get the reports I emailed you about the hotel?'

He had spun round and stood back so that she could precede him into the jet and, on the verge of answering, Caitlin stared around her in silence. Very pale, tan armchair-style seating complemented an arrangement of smooth walnut tables that could be used for dining or working. There was a concealed bar to which Javier went, also in walnut, producing two bottles of sparkling mineral water.

'Short flight,' he said. 'So no one will be serving us food, although there's champagne if you prefer it to water...'

'Water's fine,' Caitlin said hurriedly as they both went to sit, facing one another with one of the low walnut tables separating them. She launched into some spiel about the reports he had sent, on top of her game as always. Her voice was breathless and it was an effort not to just keep staring around her and soaking up the unspeakable luxury.

'We can catch up with all this when we get to the hotel,' Javier said as the plane began pushing back. 'We'll only be in the air for an hour and a half, maybe a bit more.'

Javier noted the way she clutched the arms of the chair and shot him a frozen, glassy smile. He felt a kick of satisfaction at introducing her to something that was obviously so wildly out of her comfort zone. He knew that was a purely masculine reaction, a juvenile instinct to impress, and he could almost smile at the passing weakness because it wasn't something he had ever recognised in himself.

'You can relax,' he said soothingly. 'The leather isn't going to survive that vice-like grip for very long.'

'I haven't been on anything like this before,' Caitlin confessed.

'In which case, you should sit back and enjoy the experience.'

The roar of the engines diminished when they gained height and he could hear himself think. For a few seconds, he was immersed in the moment as he looked at her.

'I used to dream of travelling.' Caitlin half-smiled. 'The furthest I got with that was travelling on a normal plane to a normal place surrounded by normal people going on a normal package holiday. You would have collapsed with shock when I went to Spain. There wasn't a single free seat, and when the guy in front decided to recline his chair I spent the rest of the flight pinned to my headrest.'

Javier's lips twitched and he smiled back at her, relaxing for the first time since he had spoken to Isabella.

'Can I ask you something?'

'Sure.'

'How is it that there's no eager guy in your life? Did one bad experience put you off men for good?'

Caitlin hesitated for a couple of seconds. She thought of the unattainable guy she had pinned her innocent fantasies on, the guy sitting opposite her with the curious expression, head tilted to one side, dark eyes capable of seeing too much for her liking. 'There *is* an eager guy in my life. He may not make the sort of demands on me that keep me from doing this or going on holiday, but he's really and truly my one great love.'

'Who?'

'Benji. He's very, very eager. Sometimes way too

eager, if I'm honest. There's only so many times a girl wants her chap jumping up on her and getting dirty paw marks all over her trousers.' Her heart was thudding as his eyes remained on her, lazy and amused. She felt he could see straight into her soul and pick out the thoughts she wanted to hide, thoughts about him and how he got to her.

'Tell me where we're heading and what's on the agenda when we get there,' she said abruptly as she broke eye contact and fumbled for her laptop. 'I can start getting to grips with the details I'll need to know before the first meeting...'

She didn't want to look at him. She was going to have to get herself together before they landed and remind herself that, whatever confidences they'd shared, she was still his employee and he was still her boss.

Things no longer felt harmless for her and it was time she began moving on.

CHAPTER SIX

CAITLIN HAD NO idea what to expect as the jet swerved lower to a view of the blue Mediterranean, curling in an arc with trees and the cluttered town sprawling behind it. Even from above, the sight was breathtaking, the absence of impersonal skyscrapers promising the old-fashioned charm of history, old architecture and atmosphere.

'You'll see why it seems like a natural place for a hotel,' Javier murmured as the jet began its descent to the airport. 'It's taken a long time for all the planning to go through, hence the importance of signing off at this last stage.'

'What would happen if you decided not to follow through and finish the deal right now?'

'It wouldn't be the end of the world.' He shrugged. 'But it would be seriously delayed and then, of course, if the fortunes of the company took a blow with the marriage falling through and news of Alfonso's ill health hitting the headlines…' He gave another shrug. 'There might have been cold feet and, with all the planning that's gone into this, it would be a very costly waste of time. Alfonso was keen to get a stake in the leisure industry here in this historic slice of Europe and, like I said, I feel duty-bound to hold my end of the bargain.'

The jet sped down with the force of a rocket landing because of its size and Caitlin gritted her teeth and regulated her breathing. She wasn't expecting Javier to reach for her hand, which was balled into a fist. He gently unclasped her fingers and linked his fingers through hers.

'Relax.'

As a ploy, it worked insofar as she was no longer focused on the jet as it dropped down at a sharp angle. How could she focus on anything but the feel of his cool fingers against hers? She stared glassy-eyed at the dark hair curling round the metal of his watch and her breath caught in her throat.

'You can give me back my hand.' She breathed. 'I'm fine.'

'I'll return it when the plane's landed.' His thumb absently rubbed hers. 'Sometimes one person's energy can rub off on someone else and I've flown on this jet a million times. I'm very calm. Are you beginning to feel a bit calmer now?'

Caitlin thankfully managed a response as her blood pressure shot through the ceiling and her eyes travelled from his wrist along his bronzed, lean and sinewy forearm.

As the jet made a soft landing, he turned to her with a smile and gently patted her hand.

'Safe and sound. You okay?'

'Perfect!'

'Good.'

He dropped her hand, sat back, and Caitlin forced herself to try and breathe normally.

Her skin burned from where it had been touched and she surreptitiously rubbed her wrist with her hand, trying to erase the tingling sensation of being branded. Her whole body tingled, as if that brief touch had ignited nerve endings everywhere inside her. She barely noticed the black four-wheel drive that waited for them as they were ushered from jet to car like royalty.

'What will you do when we get back to London?' she asked breathlessly, as soon as they were seated and the car was pulling away at a sedate pace. Nerves propelled her into speech because silence would have felt too intimate. Her body was telling her something, asking questions that she didn't feel prepared to answer.

How had this innocent crush become so overwhelming? Why hadn't it just fizzled out when Isabella had turned up, when harsh reality had intruded? How innocent was it, really?

He reclined back against the seat, his legs spread wide, one hand draped loosely over his thigh.

She licked her lips and then smiled politely when he shifted so that he was looking at her.

'Do about what?'

'Well, if your original intention was to handle Isabella's interests so that her father's illness wouldn't affect the share prices, what will happen now that the marriage has been called off? Will you still take over?'

Past him and through the window, Caitlin could see the calm, attractive panorama of palm trees fronting the sea with a deep blue sky as the backdrop. All around, there was a lack of urgency that made her feel as though she might be on holiday but, before that could take root, she killed it dead because the last thing this was, was a holiday.

'To be decided.'

Javier looked at her thoughtfully. Her skin was shiny from the heat, even though the car was air-conditioned, and her hair had gone wild. Corkscrews curled in tendrils round her heart-shaped face, her mouth slightly parted, as though she was on the verge of gasping at the scenery flashing past them. She was wearing a short-sleeved shirt, patterned with pale flowers and buttoned down the front, and a loose skirt that fell to mid-calf. It should have killed all hope of sex appeal but, the second he had seen her, her sex appeal had knocked him sideways.

He wondered now whether he had always been drawn to her on some crazy subliminal level. Had she been like a background song in his head that he only recognised now that their working relationship had shifted on its axis?

Because shifted on its axis it had, whether he wanted to admit it or not. He'd opened up to her. It was a disquieting and unsettling thought. He'd opened up to her, and had that somehow brought to the forefront an attraction he was now forced to acknowledge? A sexual pull that couldn't be indulged?

Had the different dimension to their relationship opened up a Pandora's box filled with things that couldn't be countenanced? What Caitlin wanted from life was very different from what he wanted and what he knew he would aim for. She wanted all the things he would never be able to give any woman and would never be inclined to *try* to give any woman—not to mention the small but important fact that she worked for him. Still, his eyes lowered and lingered on the fine blonde hair on her arms, her short unvarnished nails, the curve of her breasts underneath her shirt.

Aside from anything else, his days for playing the field were coming to an end. He would have to find a suitable wife, one who fitted the only lifestyle he would be able to offer, and he had a deadline. There was no Isabella around who could step up to the plate without notice, because marriage would have suited her as well and, in many ways, the later the better. He would have to spend some time finding the right woman. It wouldn't be easy.

Content with a powerful line of reasoning that was steering him away from an unacceptable temptation, Javier cast his mind back to what they were talking about—something about working in the Albarado empire. His mind wasn't on it. His mind was still trying to get off the urge to keep looking at her luscious body.

'Won't it be a little awkward?'

'Come again?' Javier frowned and dragged himself back to the present while trying to stifle the sort of tightening in his body that might be awkward to conceal.

'Even if your split was amicable, won't it be a little awkward working in her company?'

'Why would it? We're all very close to one another and always have been. The only tricky bit will revolve around a proportion of ownership. As Isabella's husband, a percentage of the shares would have devolved to me, hence there would have been more motivation on my part to make sure I had significant input into company decisions.'

'I get that. And now?'

Javier wondered what it would feel like to trail his finger over her full mouth. The feel of her small hand in his had been a powerful turn-on. Taken a couple of steps further, how much more powerful would the turn-on be? He almost groaned aloud at the disobedient tangent his mind was going down.

'Now,' he managed, 'now I'll do as much as I can and keep a close eye on Alfonso's health. He's already making small strides so that's a positive.'

'Isabella must be so relieved. Has she told him about the marriage being called off?'

'She's waiting until he's a little stronger.'

'I hope he won't be too shocked, especially considering so much was riding on your union with Isabella.'

Javier thought that the shock of the marriage being called off would take a definite second billing to the other news his daughter would soon be imparting.

'I'll continue to help out.' He brought the conversation back to its original starting point. 'But not indefinitely. I'll just paper things over until Isabella gets a handle on the nitty-gritty.'

'Can I ask you something?'

'I feel I should say no at this point.' But he smiled and continued to look at her, his eyes lazy and indulgent.

'Are you angry at Isabella for what she's done?'

'Angry?' Javier thought about it. Anger, and the loss of control it entailed, was an emotion he seldom indulged. His father's loss of control over his emotions when his wife had died had been a powerful lesson in the dangers of losing it—the dangers of letting oneself be pummelled this way and that by *feelings*. He should have been angry because, to some extent, his future had been derailed, but anger was not an emotion he could summon.

'Angry.' Caitlin half-smiled. 'As in, wanting to punch something or shout from the rooftops.'

'What would be the point of getting angry? It's not as though anger would change the circumstances. I don't do anger. And add to that list jealousy, envy and need. A life spent without those things is a richer, more rewarding life.'

'I'll bear that in mind, moving forward.' She grinned and her heart skipped a tiny beat as their eyes collided.

There was amusement in his expression and something else—something that set up a slow burn inside her, just like the burn she had felt when he had linked his fingers through hers. She was struggling to move past the warm gleam in his eyes and a tenseness in the atmosphere that gave her goose bumps.

'I mean…' she said a little weakly.

'You mean…?'

'Everyone gets angry now and again, and jealous and envious, and everyone sometimes longs for stuff they can't have but feel they need…'

'Repeat—I'm not like everyone,' Javier said softly.

'My experiences of seeing how my father reacted to my mother's loss was a lesson enough in letting emotions guide your decisions. You allow that to happen and your decisions are always going to be wrong.'

He was so close to her, Caitlin could reach out her hand and brush it against his cheek.

'Stop looking at me like that,' she whispered.

Caitlin knew what he was going to do. She felt it in her bones. He was going to kiss her, and she wanted him to, just as she had wanted to get away from talking about work and dig into his head to try and find those deeper parts she had started glimpsing. She wanted to lean against him so that she could feel his hardness against her and the steady beat of his heart under the palm of her hand pressed against his chest.

This was something that had been simmering under the surface between them for a while. She had felt it and had ignored it but it had been there, now unlocked because she was no longer just his PA. The door between them hadn't just opened for *her*. It had opened for him as well and maybe that was why she hadn't been able to kill the crush on him. Maybe she had *sensed* a spark there waiting to be lit.

Her breathing hitched and she willed him to do what she wanted him to do: kiss her; settle his mouth against hers; let his hand find the heavy weight of her breast, because her nipples were pinching against her bra and she wanted him to stop that pinching.

She should have been shocked that her beautiful boss was staring at her with hot desire, eating her with his dark eyes, but in some part of her she wasn't. Gut feeling was pushing through any sense of surprise and telling her that this was something that had been gathering momentum. If Isabella hadn't broken off the marriage, it would have come to nothing, but it had been there even when Isabella had been around because Javier hadn't been in love with his fiancée. So his eyes had wandered and she had *sensed* it.

Excitement coursed through her. A legacy of uncertainty had left her craving stability and safety when it came to any relationship with a guy. Javier was as safe and stable as a hand grenade.

But she felt an urge to see what adventure tasted like. It was one thing to read about romance and have adventures in her head but what would it really *feel like* to touch this man and have him touch her back?

Fire… She'd be putting her hand in an open flame and she would end up burnt—badly burnt.

She pulled back from the brink but she was shaking.

'This place…the scenery…amazing.'

She turned away to gaze through the window, taking in a place bathed in the last rays of early-summer sunshine. Nestled between the sea and the mountains, and curving round one of the finest bays in the country, Nice was a seductive melting pot of elegance, vibrancy and charm. The sea was very blue. As the car swerved through the streets and her mind began to calm down, she could appreciate what she had missed, the graceful architecture of some of the grand, ochre-coloured buildings. If aristocrats had flocked here once upon a time, she could understand why.

She did her best to ignore Javier's dark, disturbing

presence next to her and the tingling from her near-brush with a situation she had only just about managed to swerve.

All was forgotten as the car swept towards the hotel. It was a magnificent curving masterpiece of cream fronted by a glass-panelled arch guarded by two uniformed men. The courtyard was huge and bordered by perfectly manicured lawns on either side. Even the trees and flower-beds looked as though they had been individually seen to by a top coiffeur, not a single leaf out of place. She automatically sifted her fingers through her unruly hair and absently wondered how trees and bushes could look more precisely trimmed than *her* hair.

The people milling around were the last word in glamour, perfectly tanned with big sunglasses and designer clothes.

'This is amazing...' she breathed at yet another opulent experience.

'Not too shabby, I suppose.'

'Of course,' she said, as the uniformed guards held open the doors for them, and they left the warm sunshine to step into the cool of the white marble-and-glass foyer, 'it wouldn't be my personal choice for a honeymoon hotel. It's not exactly brimming over with romance, is it? But then, I suppose, neither was your courtship.'

'"Courtship" is a rather old-fashioned word, and there was nothing like that anyway. Can I have your passport? I'll need it to check us in.'

Caitlin reached into her handbag, handed it to him and gazed around her. Huge, ornate marble pillars intersected the expanse of cream, white and pale greys. Clusters of white upholstered chairs formed seating spaces around glass tables, and in turn were loosely partitioned off by long, oblong walnut dressers, some of which were dressed with enormous vases of white lilies.

She was vaguely aware of Javier talking to the girl behind the desk in rapid French before he turned back to her sharply.

'Right. Off we go.'

How to break the news? Javier wondered as they silently rode the lift up to their floor, because he had a feeling she was going to freak out when he told her that they would be sharing a suite of rooms, especially after their drive to the hotel. Just thinking about the sexual tension that had stretched between them made him break out in a sweat.

He'd never wanted any woman so badly in his life before. He'd known that, if he'd touched her, she would have melted in his arms, just as he'd known that giving in to that temptation would send their reliable working relationship into territory best left unexplored. She'd pulled back but he'd seen how shaky she'd been. She'd come as close as he had to turning their relationship on its head, in the grip of something as pointless as lust.

'Here we are.'

As Javier swiped the key card and stepped back, Caitlin stepped into a glorious expanse of living area. He saw her gaze past white sofas, a pale Persian rug and little glass tables, through to a veranda with yet more seating, and beyond that the fading colours of the sky that melted into a panoramic view of the sea.

She strolled towards the French doors that were flung open onto the veranda and stepped out into the balmy fresh air. There was a stupendously impressive view of a rectangular pool surrounded by neat rows of white deck chairs and white umbrellas overlooking a drop down to the ocean beneath. People were still there, drinking and being served by waiters, elegant figures in floaty sarongs and wide hats.

'Wait…' She swung round. Javier was almost directly behind her. 'Are we *both* going to be here?'

'I'm afraid so.'

'You're afraid so? I'm not sure your fear is going to help here! How is this going to work?'

'No need to look so horrified, Caitlin. It's going to work because it has to. I did ask at the desk whether two rooms would be available because of a change of circumstance but, unfortunately, the place is sold out— very popular time of year.'

'I can't share a room with you!'

'Look around you, Caitlin—this is hardly *a room*.'

'I'll stay somewhere else. It's not a problem for me. I'm not fussy.'

'Everywhere is going to be booked up.' He raked his fingers through his hair and stared at her. 'There are two bedrooms. There are two bathrooms. Our paths need not cross until a designated time in the morning when we can spend an hour or so doing our due diligence before we meet the various CEOs in the conference room reserved for us here.'

'Javier…'

'What's the problem?' His dark eyes challenged.

'What do you think is going to happen, Caitlin?' What so nearly happened between them in the back of the car hung between them, unspoken.

'Nothing's going to happen. I just...think it might be a slightly awkward situation, given it was supposed to be your honeymoon suite.'

'Isabella would have been in a separate room. This would have been a work base. You'll be in a separate room, this will be a work base. So, again...what's the problem? Because I'm comfortable with this arrangement. If an alternative had been possible, fine. But there was no alternative.'

'Isabella would have been in a separate room?'

'I told you, ours was a business arrangement in every sense of the word. So back to your objection—do you feel somehow unsafe sharing this space with me?'

Again, cool challenge was in his eyes, daring her to voice what she had no intention of voicing.

'Absolutely not.'

'Then that's nicely settled.'

He spun round on his heels and headed to the cases which had preceded them. 'Now, why don't you have a look around and settle in? I'm going to stick my case in whichever room you don't want, head downstairs, and start some preliminary liaising with the guys we'll be meeting tomorrow and confirm arrangements for the conference room. The sooner I get this wrapped up, the better.

'Isabella and I were going to meet Don, the site manager, for dinner. There's no need for you to join us but you're more than welcome, although it won't be a business meeting as such. He's an old friend of the family. You can stay here and order up food or go wherever you want to—up to you. You have the company card. Use it on whatever you choose.'

'Okay.'

'Okay to which part of what I just said?'

'Okay to being very happy to stay put and order up something to eat. Or maybe venture out. I'm not sure, but yes, I'll let you catch up with your friend and, as for the rooms, I don't mind which I get.'

'Tomorrow we can convene on the veranda at eight-thirty. I'll have breakfast brought to us.'

'Sounds good, and I'll make sure I do some final work on the deal before then.'

'Feeling a little better now about the horror of sharing this suite with me?' Half-turning to her as he strolled to retrieve his laptop from the sleek, expensive case, he raised his eyebrows, but his expression was unreadable.

'I don't remember saying anything about being horrified to share this enormous suite of rooms with you, actually.'

'Splendid, because...' he captured her gaze and held it so that she could hardly breathe '...despite what very nearly happened between us in the car, there's nothing at all to worry about.'

'I have no idea what you're talking about.'

'Of course you do.'

Caitlin felt anger roar through her because he had raised something she wanted to forget; because that brief moment, which had been earth-shattering for her, had not touched him in the same way. Her stupid crush made her vulnerable and she hated that.

'I think that's best left forgotten,' she told him coldly. 'Nothing like that has ever happened before and nothing like that will ever happen again.'

'Of course,' he murmured into the lengthening silence.

He headed for the door and repeated his invitation to spend on whatever she wanted—whether it was clothes or food, because she was doing him a favour by coming here with him—and left with a half-salute and no backward glance.

Caitlin didn't relax until she knew that Javier would no longer be in the hotel, at which point she scarpered to one of the two enormous bedrooms and firmly locked the door behind her.

She took in her surroundings, but distractedly. There was an enormous bed with crisp white linen, an enormous white sofa and a huge walnut desk, with sufficient plugs to ensure no one who wanted to work had to hunt around for charging points, and beautiful abstract paintings. The television was wafer-thin and large enough to ensure a theatrical experience. Everything was so huge and so beautiful that it was almost a shame to think about ruining it all by actually being in the room and doing stuff like going to bed or just sitting on the sofa. She could see the ocean sparkling beyond through the floor-to-ceiling French doors. Unsurprisingly, the bathroom was the size of her flat, and she and Benji could have slept in the bath with room for him to have a run.

How could she ever have foreseen this? And how

could she ever have predicted that her childish crush would morph into this great, big thing she was finding difficult to handle? She'd been hurt after Andy, and had retreated to lick her wounds, but now she could see that, even when the wounds had been well and truly licked clean, instead of getting back out there she had been lazy. She had turned her attention to Javier and idly whiled away two-plus years living in cloud cuckoo land instead of doing what any other young woman would have done—namely replacing her dead-beat ex-boyfriend with someone more suitable.

The arrival of Isabella on the scene had knocked her right back to planet Earth, but instead of propelling her into hitting the singles scene it had plunged her into the confusing place where her secret crush had grown shoots and shot up like the beanstalk in the fairy tale.

What a mess. She didn't want to be up and about when Javier returned. She needed to gather herself and take heart from the fact that they would only be here for a week. London would restore everything back to where it should be. Open doors could be shut.

With the prospect of Javier bouncing up earlier than expected from his dinner, she hurried the meal she'd ordered, which had arrived with pomp and ceremony, lots of silver domes and starched linen. She was well and truly bathed and in bed, with her door locked and only the bedside light on, when she heard the sound of the outer door being opened.

The rush of forbidden excitement, the sudden tingle of absolute awareness that he was just in the same space as her, filled her with dismay. As she switched the bedside light off, she vowed that tomorrow was another day and she would make sure to stifle all the inconvenient feelings that had no place in her relationship with her boss.

Forget about that crazy almost-moment that had nearly overtaken them. It was all in the past. And, as soon as they returned to London, she would hit the singles scene and destroy the parasite that had taken her over and was eating her up.

She just had to last out her time here and focus on the reason she had come in the first place: a missing fiancée and a deal to be delivered.

CHAPTER SEVEN

CAITLIN HAD THE day off after five days of intense meetings, with barely time to pause and think about what had turned out to be a less awkward situation than she had expected.

As arranged, they convened for breakfast first thing every morning, during which they briefed each other on what would be happening during the day, what needed to be done and what issues had to be dealt with before signing off.

On the first morning, after a restless night's sleep and with butterflies in her tummy, she had emerged from her bedroom to find Javier sitting in front of his laptop on the veranda. He'd barely glanced in her direction as she'd sat alongside him and pulled out her laptop. There'd been coffee, to which she'd helped herself, and ten minutes later various pastries and breads had been trundled in.

But for the magnificent scenery and the warmth of the sun, they could have been in his offices in London. Out of the corner of her eye, she'd glimpsed the elegant pathway below, lush green gardens on either side and the stone steps that led down between swaying palm trees to the beach in the distance. How could she not have noticed before?

Easily, she had discovered, because Javier had moved at breakneck speed through so many files and folders that she'd almost struggled to keep up with him and then, breakfast done, they had headed straight to the conference room to carry on the rest of the business at hand.

She had cleverly brought the sort of work clothes she would have actually thought twice about wearing in London—because she preferred bright, casual stuff— but, predicting an uncomfortable ambience, she had rustled up a couple of drab outfits which made her feel a bit like a fool in the balmy, laid-back surroundings.

The evenings were spent on her own while Javier did his thing with the people who would be working on the completion of the hotel deal. Five times he had issued the invitation to accompany him and five times she had politely declined, telling him she preferred to have a look around a place she'd probably never visit again.

She duly did some light exploring. She was keen but anxious, and always eager to return to the hotel before Javier so that she could avoid any conversations over a nightcap. She didn't want any more of those heady heart-to-hearts because they were too catastrophic for her nervous system. She wanted to distance herself from temptation so that things could be normal once they returned. She was desperate to bury what had happened between them.

Caitlin knew that all of that was needless worry, because Javier barely paid her a scrap of attention, reverting very easily back to being the boss and away from the guy who had linked his fingers through hers to calm her on that flight. Away from the guy who had looked at her with scorching sexual intent in his eyes.

What had been earth-shattering for her had barely registered with him as anything out of the ordinary. He might briefly have been attracted to her, but the circumstances had dictated that passing reaction more than physical lust. If he'd ever seen her in that light before then, she would have known.

It was just as well that she had pulled back from the brink of doing something both of them would regret. One touch, and he would have known that there was no way she was as casual as he was about physical contact between them.

Today, he had removed himself to have lunch with some old acquaintances who lived in Châteauneuf-du-Pape and were extensively knowledgeable on the wine grown there.

'I have a small-scale hobby on some land in southern Spain,' he had drawled, halfway out the door and before the usual breakfast routine. 'Thinking I might take it further, so a little basic info on wine growing might be in order. Don't wait up.'

'I'll try my best,' Caitlin had told him drily.

'Turn of phrase.'

She had reddened as his dark eyes had rested on her, opaque and unreadable.

'What sort of time…?' she had prompted, mentally calculating how her day would pan out in his absence.

'Very late. It's a long drive, and I intend to spend

some time enjoying the company and the town. Weather's good, and there's nothing more relaxing than gazing up at a ruined mediaeval castle with a glass of the best red waiting to be drunk. So, in short, I won't be back before ten tonight.' He'd spread his arms wide in an expressive gesture and half-smiled. 'Seize the day, as they say.'

He'd given her a mock-salute and left, and she'd breathed a sigh of heartfelt relief and got on with doing exactly as he'd instructed.

Nice was famous for its museums. She took one in and then strolled in the mild summer warmth, enjoying the sights, smells, chatter in different tongues and the rapid, romantic French accent as people strolled past her. She grabbed lunch but was too eager to carry on sight-seeing to sit still for long and, by the time mid-afternoon rolled round, she had managed to explore Old Nice with its narrow cobblestone streets and buildings in pale pastel hues, enjoying all the cheeses and breads spilling from stalls and the huge array of flowers that filled the air with an aroma that was fragrant and seductive.

Never in her wildest dreams, in foster care, had she thought that the experience of being somewhere else could feel so wonderful and so alien at the same time.

Once she became tired of walking, the hotel pool became irresistible, perched up above the ocean with its elegant array of shaded loungers and precision-straight umbrellas. People were lazily sunbathing, but there were many empty loungers, and it was bliss to while away a couple of hours soaking up the sun.

Javier wasn't going to be back until very late. She'd actually checked how far the place was, and he'd be several hours on the road, never mind sipping red wine and catching up with old friends while gazing at a mediaeval castle. All that stuff took time. He would be very lucky to be home by midnight, she reckoned.

Caitlin had never envied the lifestyle of the rich and famous—the opposite, if anything. She had occasionally seen some of the women Javier dated, and had often wondered—how much time went into the business of being impeccably groomed? How much time was spent hunting down the perfect outfits to grab the attention of a guy who was never going to be in it for the long haul? What effort was involved in trying to impress the world? It must be exhausting.

But, here, she guiltily saw what serious money got a person when it came to sheer luxury: poolside staff jumping to attention; a list of cocktails as long as her arm served with melt-in-the-mouth snacks; loungers she could fall asleep on; and the quiet hush of very expensive people who never did rowdy things such as yell, shout or dive into the pool irrespective of whether they splashed anyone.

It was bliss, quite frankly. She was a couple of mojitos down by the time six o'clock rolled round and she headed back to the suite. Pleasantly relaxed, and relishing the freedom of being able to strip off and walk around in the buff safe in the knowledge that Javier wouldn't be around for hours, Caitlin reminded herself that she was really going to commit to embracing her singledom just as soon as she returned to London. For the moment, however, as she flung on a thin, sheer sarong—which was just about okay for sitting on the veranda, because there was nothing at all underneath—she had not a thought in her head except for the mind-fulness of the moment.

The intensity of the sun was fading. Down below, if she was to look over the railings of the veranda, she would see the very pool she had just left, but from here, half-dozing with a bottle of water in one hand, all she could see from the cushioned chair was the blue sky and ocean and the fine, dark line dividing the two.

She nodded off to the pleasant background sound of the breeze and the distant sea and the even more distant sounds of people below, thinning out at the pool as the light began to fade.

When she started at a sudden noise and looked at her phone it was only just seven—loads of time to take it easy before she catapulted into fifth gear and made sure she was in her bedroom by the time her boss returned.

And tomorrow would be the perfect time to get round to all her good intentions.

Javier let himself into a silent space. It was a little after seven-fifteen and he still wasn't entirely convinced as to why he had changed his plans for the day. He'd set off with great intentions to enjoy some downtime whilst also quizzing his grizzled, humorous friend about vine-yards and wine production. He would inherit his vine-yards by hook or by crook and, once he did, a little useful information would come in handy.

But he'd been filled with a vague restlessness as soon as he'd left the hotel. The past five days had stretched his willpower to breaking point. He was in the unique position of knowing that a woman wanted him, knowing that he wanted her just as much, yet powerless to do anything about the situation because Caitlin was out of bounds.

Much more than that, though—she was complicated. He thought of her having been in foster care…all the sadness that would have gone with that…the faith in love and romance that it had engendered against all odds, the desire for security.

The last guy she needed was someone like him, whether he was her boss or not. He was not going to go there, whatever erotic fantasies he had going on in his head…was he?

With all sorts of problems looming on the horizon— from marriage plans going down the plug hole, to an expiry date on his freedom if he was to get control of the vineyards he was so desperate to have—there was more than enough to worry about. Instead, the only thing he was able to think of was whatever was going on between Caitlin and himself.

He hated to think that he was the sort of guy who could crave what he couldn't have but, ever since that almost crazy moment, he had watched her out of the corner of his eye, watched her every movement, and had gritted his teeth against a libido that threatened to rocket into the stratosphere.

When he lay in bed at night, he practically groaned aloud at the thought of her lying in a bed within touching distance of him. How was he supposed to have talked wine, drunk wine and whiled away several hours in the sun without itching to get back to the hotel? Which was why he had met Jean-Paul halfway, enjoyed a light lunch with him, caught up on news, while only glancing at his watch four times, and then made his way back to the hotel earlier than intended.

Last day in Nice… He'd planned to avoid all temptation, but something had got the better of his usual impeccable judgement, and now here he was, in the suite…

Javier drew in a sharp breath as he moved towards the veranda just as she lazily stood up with her back to him.

What was she wearing? What was she *not* wearing? Where was the attraction-killing work garb she had been keen to wear for the past few days? The thin wisp of fabric swathed around her showed everything he'd fantasised about for the past five days: round backside, shapely legs, narrow waist…

She was moving back inside, staring at her phone, and smiling as the sarong blew open. Javier went rock-hard in seconds. He felt his urgent erection pushing against his linen trousers. He couldn't have peeled his eyes away from the luscious sight in front of him if he'd tried. Her breasts hung like ripe fruit waiting to be tasted, her nipples large orbs, pink and perfectly defined, begging to be sampled.

Dios mío!

Caitlin was moving forward towards a sound that had barely registered, smiling at the picture Angie had sent her of Benji, until she glanced up, and for a few seconds her mind went blank.

She had a sluggish déjà vu, a flashback to standing on that chair with a wedding dress on, but this time, as reality returned in a rush, she knew that it was much, much worse.

She stared down and saw the nakedness of her breasts and the panties that barely covered anything. She felt every inch of her body; felt the rush of blood through her veins, the tickle of wetness spreading between her thighs and the sensitive tightening of her nipples as they scraped against the thin sarong.

'What are you doing here? What the *heck* are you doing here?' She scrambled to get herself presentable.

'I...' Javier raked his fingers through his hair and glanced away, but not for long.

'You shouldn't be here!' Caitlin screeched. 'And... *don't*. Just...*don't*!'

'Don't what?'

'Don't you *dare* look at me like that!'

'Like what, Caitlin? Tell me! No, you don't have to tell me. You don't want me to look at you as if you're the only woman on earth; as if I want to do nothing more than rip that flimsy bit of cloth off so that I can do what I've been wanting to do for too long now.'

'You don't mean that!'

'Damn right I mean it—every word. Wanting to touch you has been driving me crazy.'

'You're my boss! I'm not your type. *You're* not my type... We've all but *agreed* that!'

Silence fell, an electric silence thrumming with everything that was unspoken, charged with *want*.

'In that case...'

Javier began turning away and, in that split-second, Caitlin had a soaring insight into her life, her choices, her past, her present and her future. She saw all the dreams she'd had in her foster home: romantic dreams of frothy weddings, babies and happy-ever-afters. She'd lost herself in those dreams. They had been her escape and, for a while with Andy, she'd projected those dreams onto him and pretended that he could be 'the one' for her. Her disillusionment had pulled her into a place of safety. She'd looked at her boss and taken refuge in a crush that had never been able to come to anything but, in doing so, she had removed herself from real life with all its complications, dangers and chances that she could have taken.

Somewhere in her head, she had decided that chances weren't for her. But here she was, and she was suddenly driven to take the biggest chance of all.

What would it feel like just to give in to temptation? Could she live in the moment without looking ahead to regret? With Javier, she knew what she would be getting into, and that would be nothing—nothing at all. Wasn't that safer, in a way—taking the plunge without spinning castles in the sky about a future that was never going to happen?

'Wait…' Heart in her mouth, she reached out and circled his wrist with her hand, while she clutched the sarong tightly together with the other.

Javier stilled.

Every muscle in his body froze at the branding touch of her fingers on his skin and the hesitant tone in her voice. He looked at her with hunger. If he'd ever thought for a single moment that he'd known what it felt like to play with fire, then he'd been wrong. *This* was playing with fire.

'What am I waiting for? Tell me!'

'I'm not sure! I'm confused! I don't understand. I'm so attracted to you but I know that it would be stupid to do anything about it. *Dumb!*'

'You think I don't know that?'

'I don't know what to do! This is all your fault!'

'You think *I'm* not confused?' He raked restless fingers through his hair.

'We should walk away from this. It doesn't make sense.'

'If we do, will what we feel, this charge between us that's come from nowhere, conveniently leave us alone? Or will curiosity never let either of us go? And, if that's the case, how will it impact our working relationship down the road? Think about it.'

Javier half-turned away, because if he carried on looking he knew that he would find it impossible not to reach out…smooth those strands of hair from her cheeks…trace the delectable hollow of her cleavage… reach down and kiss her full mouth…

'I'm trying to think, Javier, but you make it pretty hard to keep a clear head.'

'Okay, so how about this?' he said shakily. 'Whatever happens tonight happens or doesn't happen. That's your call. Either way, we leave tomorrow and, once we're back in London, whether this thing is still there between us or not, we will never talk about it again—ever.'

'Okay.'

Okay? *Okay?* Frustration tore through him, but there

was no way he would do anything to make her feel uncomfortable or to jeopardise the terrific relationship they had fostered over the years. He respected her too much for that, even though he'd never felt so turned on in his life before.

When he harnessed his wayward thoughts, it was to find that she had turned away and was heading towards her bedroom, closing the door on him.

He wanted her!

Caitlin lay in bed with her eyes wide open, staring up at the ceiling as the minutes and hours ticked by. She played and replayed every word of what he had said and analysed every expression on his face she remembered until her head was spinning. Her whole body ached from the desire she was desperate to subdue, because of course they were both right in acknowledging that this...*thing*...between them had to be ignored. So what if curiosity ate away at them? If they mutually agreed never to mention it again, then curiosity would surely fade over time.

Except, what would happen to all these feelings that had been unleashed inside her? It would be easy for Javier to move past a brief attraction generated by the unusual physical circumstances in which they found themselves, with her a heartbeat away in a honeymoon suite. But would it be equally easy for her?

He had no idea of the fantasies trapped in her head about him, fantasies woven over time, carefully nurtured while she'd foolishly avoided the singles scene. Would those fantasies become more strident when they returned to London, when her eyes followed him as he moved in the office? Would her body yearn to take what was on offer here, an offer which would no longer be on the table the minute they returned to the reality of the outside world? Would sleeping with him finally kill off an inconvenient desire?

She had hours to decide—less. She knew that he would respect whatever she chose to do because that was the kind of guy he was.

As the thoughts buzzed in her head like angry insects, she wished that she could be better prepared to handle a situation like this but, whilst making her resilient in many ways, the strange world of foster care had left her curiously vulnerable in others.

It was a little after ten when she decided that checking the fridge for something to eat might be a good idea. She couldn't stay lying on the bed a minute longer. She was overthinking and needed to move. She knew that the fridge was ridiculously well-stocked with chocolates, biscuits, bottles of water and interesting packets of various French cheeses.

But how did her feet manage to pause outside Javier's bedroom door en route to getting something from that fridge? How did her hand end up pushing open his door— a door that had been left invitingly ajar? And how did her feet softly pad to where he was turning in the bed?

Her heart was thudding and the feverish thoughts had coalesced into one, overpowering realisation: *she was going to do this. She had to do this.*

The life in her imagination had always been colourful, but that had never mirrored reality, and the reality was that she had always been risk-averse. She had always thought that daring adventures of the heart were meant for other people, but not for her.

She'd always assumed that her need for safety was too ingrained for her to jeopardise it by taking chances—especially after Andy, who had been a terrible error of judgement.

But with Javier... The error of judgement would be to deny what her body wanted and shy away from this driving need greedily to take what he offered.

'You came.'

Caitlin hovered. She was a lot more covered than she had been when she'd worn her sarong—she was modestly attired in a baggy tee-shirt and long pyjama bottoms—yet she felt more exposed now than she had with less on. She felt stripped bare under the hooded gaze of those dark eyes—stripped bare and unspeakably excited.

'I came.'

'I'm glad you did.'

'Were you expecting me?' Her voice was shaky and barely a whisper.

'Come a little closer and I'll tell you.'

Should she confess to him just how innocent she was when it came to sex? That was a thorny conversation she had never rehearsed in any of her make-believe scenarios.

He was now sitting up, watching her with lazy interest as she came closer, and he patted the space next to him.

'I wasn't expecting anything, I was hoping—hence I left the door ajar.'

'To tempt me in?'

'Should you be passing,' he murmured with a crooked smile. 'To give you something to think about. Come, climb in. It's a lot warmer under the covers with me than it is standing there.'

Her inexperience roared through her like a gale-force wind, filling her with a tremor of apprehension, but she shuffled towards the bed, took a deep breath, half-closed her eyes and did as he'd asked. She slipped under the soft duvet which he had raised obligingly for her.

Oh, good heavens...

The feel of his nakedness sent her blood pressure soaring and she gasped and closed her eyes. He slowly ran his hand over the tee-shirt, then under it, and she trembled when his fingers found the stiffened bud of her nipple and began to stroke. She was in the moment and yet outside it, looking down at herself in wonderment at what was happening.

It was surreal. The wetness between her thighs was shocking, as was the raw need for him to put his hand there and soothe the restless, demanding tingle that was driving her crazy.

He pushed up the tee-shirt and she opened her eyes a crack to watch as he straddled her with his big, muscular body, absently touching himself before easing down to suckle on a tender nipple.

Caitlin groaned. Pleasure exploded inside her. She could barely breathe as a new world was unleashed, a world of dizzying sensation and mind-blowing excitement.

The adventures in her head were tame compared to the tumult of sensation racing through her, igniting every corner of her responsive body. She arched up, wanting more of his mouth on her. She didn't want him to take his time. She wanted him to be in a hurry so that this weird, wonderful, crazy craving was satisfied immediately! Instinct made her reach down to touch herself but he didn't even lift his mouth from her nipple as he stayed her hand.

She felt him murmur something against her breast and groaned. By the time he rose from his thorough exploration of her breasts, she could barely contain her escalating pleasure, and it took just one touch from him, just the slide of his fingers over her clitoris, for her whole body to burst into orgasm.

She cried out and spasmed, not caring a jot that his eyes were on her, watching her come.

'Oh, Javier!' She gave a long, shuddering moan.

'Good God, you're so damned beautiful.'

Caitlin reached to squeeze him tightly as he subsided next to her on the mattress. 'So are you. God, so was *that*. I've never… Oh, Javier… I'm sorry.'

'For what?'

'For…not lasting a little longer but…but…'

'But what, *querida*?'

Caitlin squirmed from where she had burrowed against his neck and looked at him anxiously. Her body was calmer but she could still feel the heat inside her, ripples of sexual awareness making her warm and tender.

'Javier, I don't want you to freak out.'

'Just saying that is making me freak out. What is it?'

'I… I've never done this before.'

'Never done…*what*?'

Caitlin looked at him defensively. 'I knew you'd freak out. I knew you wouldn't want this!'

She began turning away, humiliated in advance at the prospect of doing the walk of shame to the bedroom door, dishevelled and semi-undressed. Why had she said anything? She could have faked it and he would have been none the wiser but, as it stood, why on earth would he want to make love to someone with zero experience? How would that be a good time for him?

'Caitlin…'

'Don't say anything,' she ordered shakily. 'I know it's not what you expected…'

'You're a virgin.'

'It's not a crime.'

'Look at me.'

Caitlin raised cautious, challenging eyes to his. In the semi-darkness, there was amused tenderness in his gaze and something soft fluttered inside her.

'You're not…disappointed?'

Staring deep into her eyes, Javier realised that he couldn't think of a single word further removed from 'disappointed' to describe how he felt right now.

A virgin. He had never sought one out and, if asked, would have said that the prospect of sleeping with a virgin would have him running for the hills, because it smacked of the sort of complications he would never touch with a bargepole. Now, though, as he looked into her hesitant, defiant, hopeful gaze, he wanted her with a ferocity that shocked him.

'Far from it,' he murmured huskily, an understatement to beat all understatements. 'It makes me want to show you everything, *querida*. It makes me want your sweet, responsive body in ways I can't even begin to describe—and, trust me, I'll be gentle with you. When I enter you, you'll open up to me like a flower, and I promise to take you to heights you can't begin to imagine.'

'That's a lot of big promises.' There was a shaky smile in her voice.

'And I intend to keep every one of them…'

True to his word, Javier took it slow. He stripped her with the delicacy of someone handling priceless porcelain and, when she was stretched out in front of his devouring gaze, naked and breathtakingly beautiful, he forgot his own needs and devoted every ounce of attention to making this the best experience of her life.

He linked his fingers through hers, held her hands above her head and explored her breasts, revelling in their lush abundance, lathing the orbs of her nipples with his tongue until she was wriggling and moaning.

He delighted in the little mewling noises she made as he traced a sensuous contour along her ribcage with his tongue, moving lower to circle her belly-button. He took his time, even though it was agonising, because his body was on fire.

He reared up as his wandering mouth, tongue and fingers reached the sexy crease of her womanhood. She was flushed, eyelids trembling, her mouth softly parted on an expectant sigh.

For a few seconds, Javier was overwhelmed. His life had been prescribed for so long that this felt like an adventure—a thrilling, dangerous adventure with no signposts to follow.

She made a tiny urging sound, and he smiled then levered himself in just the right position to swing her legs over his shoulders. He breathed her in, nostrils flaring at the musky feminine scent. Delicately he slid his tongue between that damp crease and found the throbbing bud of her clitoris with no trouble. He was determined that the next time she orgasmed it would be with him inside her, deep, hard and moving at just the right pace to take her over the edge.

He did things slowly, teasing her with his tongue, getting her high on *want*, and then, when he knew that he would come himself if he didn't do what his body clamoured for him to do, he reached for protection, sheathed himself and took her.

CHAPTER EIGHT

JAVIER LOOKED AT CAITLIN, who was moving around the bedroom in search of clothing that had been scattered earlier en route from door to bed. It was a matter of a few paces but after an excellent meal, that had gone on for way too long in his opinion, they had been so desperate to rip each other's clothes off that there were items of clothing everywhere.

Worth the haste, though, he mused now with intense satisfaction as he watched her hold a sock in one hand and her bra in the other. He'd propped himself up on one elbow, all the better to appreciate the swing of her heavy breasts as she padded naked across the room. Her hair was dishevelled and he clocked the sway of her peach bottom… Incredibly, he could feel himself hardening again.

They'd prolonged their stay. That first night had been amazing, explosive, revelatory and, more to the point, not enough for either of them.

She'd lain in his arms and he'd stroked her hair and been tickled pink as she waxed lyrical about how fantastic the experience had been.

They explored the city to within an inch of its life.

She'd barely travelled, and he enjoyed showing her around the famous museums, strolling through the old town, with its charming streets and colourful buildings, and pausing for lunch on the promenade surrounded by tourists with the warm sun pouring down on them like honey, making them lazy and hot for one another.

For Javier, life was on hold, and he was enjoying it. Why not? Problems lay round the corner and there would be time enough to deal with them when this madness was over: Isabella; her situation; the company that would need at least some steering whether he was her husband or not; and of course the timeline for his own marriage, which wasn't going to go away, because he wasn't ready for it.

He thought of Caitlin—her joyous innocence, her sweetly responsive body that was always eager for his touch…

He wanted to lose himself in a holiday from reality and enjoy what he would never have again because his journey now would be with another suitable wife to replace the empty spot left by his vanishing fiancée.

Of course, he'd been astute enough to remind her that this was just time out for them, nothing serious, just fun. He'd sidelined any concerns that had sprung to mind when she had confessed that she'd been a virgin. He'd buried them under the fact that she knew him, and knew what he wanted in a woman, because he'd made it clear over the time they'd been here.

She'd met Isabella, so she would be in no doubt that the woman he eventually sought for his wife would be of a similar mould. She'd said as much, unprompted by him.

If he'd omitted the fact that there was a timeline governing finding this woman yet to appear on the scene, then that had simply been a courtesy. He fancied that she was enjoying him, and enjoying the bubble they were in, and would hardly want it burst before its time.

He fancied that he was doing her a favour, when he got right down to it. With him, she was preparing herself for the reality of life in which sex and lust didn't necessarily lead to love and marriage. She would emerge tougher and stronger, more capable of protecting herself against men like the boyfriend who had broken her heart.

His thoughts did what they always seemed to do when he was with her—strolled off in the opposite direction. Lying back just as he was now—naked and stirring into pleasant arousal, appreciating her voluptuous curves— he would suddenly catch himself idly imagining the sort of guy she should end up with. And found the whole idea of it vaguely distasteful.

'Is it just me or are you getting a little bored here?'

'Here, as in the bedroom, right now? I'm…not bored, no, but I'm a little hungry.'

Javier glanced at his phone on the bedside table and realised that it was now a little past seven-thirty in the evening. They'd been in bed for a staggering amount of time. How had *that* happened? he wondered. He frowned and swept aside a stirring of unease.

'Now that you mention it, so am I. It's later than I thought.'

'I guess we've been busy.'

Their eyes tangled and again he felt something stir inside him, something a little bit unwelcome, a tenderness that seemed to leave her and find a connection in him.

'It's time to get out of here,' he drawled. 'And no need to go with the bra, by the way. I like the weight of your breasts in my hands. I like being able to touch and feel your nipples harden.'

He grinned with wolfish intent and enjoyed the way she went red and was momentarily lost for words. His addled head cleared.

'Get out and go where?'

When she looked at him, she felt that familiar surge of sexual charge, but this time it was mixed with a flare of sudden panic because she knew that she was living on borrowed time with this beautiful, wonderful guy.

One night! That was all it was meant to be. She had crept into his bedroom, nerves shredded but overcome with the sort of mad desire she'd never thought herself capable of feeling, and they had made love. She'd been scared that her lack of experience might turn him off, but it had been just the opposite. The minute he'd touched her, her body had burst into flames and now…? Now she knew that he held her in his hands like a puppet master. The crush had turned into something fierce and raw, and it was more than physical. He'd captured every bit of her, from her body to her soul. She'd fallen for him, and she wondered whether she hadn't fallen for him a long while back, because he was just so much more than the sum of all his parts. Barriers had been broken down and, in this wonderful bubble, he had become her world. It didn't matter that he had warned her off wanting more than he was prepared to give.

As she glanced over her shoulder, she could see that what she'd felt for Andy had been a pale shadow of what she felt for Javier. But, then again, working for him, alongside him, getting to know him in a million different, little ways… Her heart had been lost a long time ago and she hadn't even realised it.

Of course, she couldn't carry on working for him when they returned to London, so this time here was precious. The longer they extended their stay, the happier she was. She would deal with the chaos of her emotions when it ended and she walked away from him for good.

It was a struggle to meet his intense, dark gaze without giving away her thoughts. She didn't dare raise the topic of returning to London. If he raised it, then fine, but she wasn't going to pre-empt anything.

She found that she was holding her breath and, at risk of going blue in the face, she hissed it out slowly.

'No need to look so worried, but I think it's time to move on.'

'Oh, really?' Her heart sank but she kept her cool and maintained his stare.

'We've done the cafés and the jazz club and the museums, and exclaimed sufficiently at the ocean and the scenery.'

Caitlin maintained a mute silence whilst surreptitiously gathering her clothes from the ground and trying to shield her nakedness. Naked and serious, life-altering conversation didn't seem to go hand in hand.

'Change beckons,' Javier drawled, flinging the covers aside and treating her to the magnificent sight of his bronzed, muscle-packed body.

'So it does,' she said faintly.

'And I know that there's frankly a ton of work waiting to be done, amongst other duties too many to mention.' He strolled towards her, relieved her of the bra, held it up while maintaining eye contact and grinned. 'Tut, tut. What have I said about not liking you wearing a bra?'

'And back in the day, when dinosaurs ruled the world, that sort of macho talk might have meant something...' Her voice was more tart than she'd intended.

'Don't tell me you don't love it when I do this...'

Caitlin breathed in sharply and shuddered as he reached to cup her breasts and then roll his thumb over her stiffened nipple. She flung back her head, felt wetness begin to spread between her thighs, and her arms went limp. She could *feel* his hot satisfaction as he stroked her nipple between his fingers, while with his other hand he reached down to cup her wetness.

He slid fingers into her and teased a devastating response. Caitlin dropped everything she'd been clutching and clutched him instead as her whole body quivered. She barely recognised the guttural moan that emerged as his rhythm got quicker and firmer over her throbbing clitoris until she could no longer contain the orgasm splintering through her.

She arched back and groaned, eyes squeezed tightly

shut, and the high colour of sexual gratification scorched her cheeks.

He caught her as she subsided like a rag doll against him, their naked bodies pressed hard against one another. She felt his hardness against her and reached down to circle it. It was his turn this time.

He'd taught her well. When she glanced down, forehead pressed against his chest, she thrilled at the sight of his impressive brown member and the slightness of her pale fingers circling it. She could feel the pulse of his arousal and, as she worked her own magic, she never took her eyes off him as, like her, he came to a shuddering orgasm.

'I think we're both due a bath,' he rasped into her hair, and she looked up at him and blinked, already careering into the conversation they'd left behind when touching had become more urgent than talking.

'Why are you looking at me like that?' he asked with a frown.

'Like what?'

'Like you're worried about something.'

'I always get worried when I'm hungry.' Caitlin glanced down to escape the penetrating intensity of his gaze. 'One day I'll get to grips with a rigid diet, and then I'll be able to laugh in the face of semi-starvation.' She was keeping it light but her heart was pounding like a sledgehammer as he drew back from her, held her at arm's length and just looked until she reluctantly returned the stare.

'Promise me you'll never do that,' he said seriously.

'Do what?' Her voice was bewildered.

'Go on any diet, rigid or otherwise. You're beautiful just the way you are.'

'If you say so.'

'I do. I love making love to you, feeling your body under my hands, your curves… I think I've already proved that. In fact, I'd say that particular record is on permanent repeat.'

Caitlin thought that 'permanent' was an adjective that couldn't be further from the truth. 'Permanent' was the one thing he'd reminded her more than once that he would never do.

She turned, breaking the connection, and walked towards the en suite, aware of him padding softly behind her.

'I'd go for the bath option,' he said with lazy amusement, reaching to turn on the waterfall shower which, in its vast wet-room space, was easily big enough for both of them and then some. 'But I think we both need to eat. I can hear my own stomach protesting from lack of food.'

They showered together. It wasn't the first time. But this time her head was cluttered as she tried to make sense of what was going on.

Was he going to try and persuade her to carry on what they had when they returned to London? She would, naturally, decline the kind offer if that turned out to be the case but no way would she hint about the resignation she was determined to hand in. Or maybe he was going to call it a day. That being the case, he was very upbeat, but then again he wasn't emotionally involved. She was just someone else who'd come along in the void left by Isabella.

Tension made her stomach tighten as she flung on some clothes. She'd bought some stuff in a couple of the little independent shops. Javier had tried to urge her into some of the more expensive boutiques, but she had laughed and turned down the offer.

'Where will we go for something to eat?' She broke the silence as they headed out.

'Somewhere small and quiet so that we can talk.'

'We do need to do that,' Caitlin said tensely while her heart continued to beat a frantic tempo and her brain scrambled over possible scenarios, none of which had a happy ending. 'There's a ton of work stuff piling up, as you said. I've actually tried to clear some emails over the past couple of days.'

'As have I. We can get to the work chat later. Right now, let's try and find somewhere to eat.'

'You…mentioned that it was time to move on,' she forced herself to say as they stepped into another balmy evening and walked out towards the bustling shops and cafés.

'I did. Like I said, I think it's time to move on from Nice, and I have a proposition.'

'No.'

'Come again?'

Caitlin was warming up to what was coming. She carried on walking briskly but then slowed up when he tugged her to his side, pulling her to a stop.

'Let's find somewhere to sit so that we can have this conversation,' he said quietly.

The minute he'd uttered those words about having a proposition, she'd known where he was going. She'd worked alongside him long enough to be wise to his dating habits. He enjoyed women, and treated them like queens just until his interest started to wane, at which point they were politely but firmly ushered out. Isabella might be no more, but Caitlin would stake her life's savings on her boss returning to his previous lifestyle.

Was she going to be like all those other women? No. Her heart just wouldn't be able to stand it. She lacked their experience, and the line between fun and misery would be an easy one to cross. She intended to have her say before he could use any persuasive tactics on her. She was weak around him, but being weak wasn't going to do. She had to assert authority over the situation or risk even greater heartbreak by being persuaded into ditching the resignation and continuing an affair with the guy she worked for.

How easy it would be, working by day with the slow build of excitement racing in her veins as she anticipated a night with him…the accidental brush of his hand on her arm…dark eyes lingering just a little too long. It would be clandestine, thrilling, decadent…

And way too dangerous for someone whose dream had always been to be safe in a relationship.

She had no regrets about making the choice she had made. How could she? But she couldn't afford to layer it up with complications she would find impossible to deal with.

'So…' Javier mused, just as soon as they'd found a suitable restaurant, having strolled there in silence. 'You're suddenly very serious, *querida*. You haven't heard what

I'm going to say and you've decided that you want no part of it?'

'I know what you're going to say.'

'Really? I'm shocked. I had no idea you were gifted in the art of mind-reading.'

'Work calls,' Caitlin said wryly. 'And it's time for us to return to London. In all the time I've worked for you, I've never known you to take spontaneous time off, so I'm guessing you've got itchy feet. How am I doing so far?'

'I'm curious to hear where the story is going.'

Caitlin's heart fluttered. Why did he have to be so stupidly gorgeous, so incredibly clever, witty and perceptive? So *unavailable*?

'You and Isabella are no longer together…'

'Ten out of ten for observational accuracy.' He grinned, raised his eyebrows and slid a glance at her. 'What comes next?'

'And we've had a good time here. Unexpected—not a good idea, but…'

'Agree on all counts.'

'I won't continue this situation once we return to London. It would be untenable.'

There, she'd said it. She thought about walking out of his life for good and gritted her teeth. Tough situations demanded tough choices. Would he miss her—the person he'd grown to know aside from the employee without the back story? 'You're not the kind of guy I'm looking for as a partner and, whilst this is fun, it's really opened my eyes to the importance of getting on with my life.'

'Getting on with your life?'

'Finding the guy who's right for me. You were my adventure, and it was good that I...that we... It wasn't a mistake, put it that way.'

'That's very gratifying, and should I be flattered that you considered me a stepping stone in your ambition to find yourself Mr Right, or offended? Or *insulted* even?'

Caitlin reddened. Was he teasing her? Was he less bullet-proof than she'd always thought?

'I've hurt you and I'm sorry.'

'I'm kidding, Caitlin. Of course you haven't hurt me, so don't worry about that. I'm thicker skinned than you think. No, I get what you're saying one hundred percent.' He leant forward, elbows on the table, and steepled his fingers. 'We've already established that when it comes to longevity you're no more my type than I am yours. You want all sort of things a man like me could never provide, aside from which...'

'Aside from which...?'

Javier hesitated. He'd already told her enough about himself—too much. Why launch into his need to get hold of vineyards, what he had to do to get them to fulfil his dream of owning a slice of his past tied up in memories of joy and happiness? Why repeat what she already knew? That the lessons from his past could never be undone. That he would tie the knot with someone who understood his limitations.

'You had a rough time growing up, and I can understand why you've invested so much in finding love with the right guy, and that's fine. If I'm your adventure on the way to getting there, then that's also fine.'

'Will you…?' Caitlin hesitated but what did she have to lose? They'd already crossed a million lines, and besides, she would be handing in her resignation as soon as she got to London so there would be no repercussions from anything she might decide to ask him now. No awkward moments.

'Will I what?'

'Will you still have a business-like marriage, with some other suitable candidate?'

'Yes.'

'How can you be so sure?'

'I know myself and I know what I want and what I need.'

He'd said that before and yet she still felt a stab of pain because she was forced to accept what her heart didn't want: his casualness; his affection that was only skin-deep; the fact that she was disposable, however much he liked her, and however many laughs and confidences they shared.

'What I meant—' she smiled stiffly '—is whether you think you're destined to marry someone else who has a company you would like to merge with yours.'

'No immediate candidates spring to mind. Why are we talking about this?'

'I don't know how we got there. I suppose I'm curious.'

'Well, if it satisfies your curiosity…' He dropped his voice, topping up both glasses with wine and leaning towards her in a way that was confidential and intimate, making her skin tingle. 'I'm not completely ruthless when it comes to choosing a woman I'd want to spend my life with.'

'What does that mean?'

'It means I would never marry any woman because of her financial holdings.' He grinned. 'I have plenty of my own. Isabella and I had something that went beyond that. We had family loyalties and tangled duties and a shared history, along with the weight of familial expectations, not to mention a list of other reasons all vying for airtime.'

'So then what on earth would you be looking for?'

'Let's stay in the present,' he drawled. 'This is a dead-end topic.'

'It's only dead-end because you don't want to talk about it.'

'It's dead-end because it's not relevant to what I want to say.' He sighed, impatient and indulgent at the same time. '*Querida*, you know the sort of woman I'll end up with. Someone who doesn't need of huge amounts of attention. Someone who will be able to ease comfortably into a lifestyle of making sure everything is running efficiently on the home front, and also being able to effortlessly deal with the socialising that will come with the terrain.

'It would also help, I suppose, if she came from a similar background to mine. Spanish high society is slightly different than its equivalent here, and as and when I take over my father's business interests I expect

I'll end up splitting my time between London and Madrid. There won't be much time for on-the-job training.'

'Perhaps you might need a training manual of sorts for whoever gets the job,' Caitlin said. 'I could get one put together for you.'

How could he say all this stuff, utter sentiments that couldn't be further from what she expected out of life, and yet capture her heart and soul without even trying? Eager to get away from this diversion, she dug into the prawn salad, made suitable noises about it being delicious and then reconfirmed what she had earlier said about having no intention of continuing what they had just because they still happened to be attracted to one another.

'This...all of this...' She drank some of the wine and looked at him evenly. 'Is wonderful.'

'Got it—your personal adventure before you find the real thing. No need to labour the point... And yes, it's been good, I won't deny that.'

'Well, that's sorted, then. We agree.'

Javier looked at her steadily. 'I agree,' he told her flatly. 'About London. When we return, it would be difficult for us to return to the right balance if this continued—too many blurred lines. Which is why I'm not proposing that we do any such thing.'

'You're not?'

'I'm not.' He smiled slowly and sat back, pushing his plate to one side and looking at her for a few seconds in contented silence. 'What I'm proposing is this: we leave here and head somewhere else. This was a work destination, after all, and the work's been concluded. We've had fun here, but I want us to go where we won't be interrupted. Somewhere where we can make love whenever we like and get this thing we have between us out of our systems before real life beckons.'

He made it sound so simple. As if what they had between them was no bigger than a passing infection, easily killed off with some antibiotics, never to resurface again. They couldn't have been more on different pages.

'What are you suggesting?' she asked carefully.

'Maybe a week or two on my yacht.'

Whilst Caitlin knew everything there was to know about the company holdings, she knew next to nothing about his own private possessions. Yes, he owned several priceless paintings. She had once had to renew the eye-watering insurance on them, because his private fund manager had been in hospital, but for the rest she had not a clue, really.

'Your yacht…'

'Which is conveniently moored at the moment off Monaco. We could do some perfunctory sightseeing there and then decamp to the yacht which, let me assure you, is far from ostentatious. You could say it's in the same league as a handy run-around car when you don't want to bring out the Bentley.'

'I doubt it's the equivalent of my run-around car.'

Caitlin was already thinking ahead to a few more snatched moments with Javier. She gazed off into the distance and rapidly worked out pros and cons. It was all pros and no cons, as far as she was concerned. She'd committed to this wonderful bubble for as long as it continued. She'd accepted that she would resign once the bubble had burst because there was no way she could continue working for a guy she was madly in love with, watching while he picked up where he'd left off with other women; arranging dates for him to fancy places with his trademark catwalk-model girlfriends. Until such time as the perfect accessory came along, suitable for marriage and living the life expected of Spanish aristocracy.

But in the meantime she was on this adventure. She would pick up the pieces later and she knew that, when she did, she would be all the more determined that safety was what she wanted, but at least she would have got the heady adventure out of the way. She was only doing what most girls did! She'd just taken her time getting there and had had to jump one enormous hurdle along the way.

'You're looking thoughtful.'

Caitlin blinked and focused on Javier, who was staring at her with an expression she couldn't quite read.

Capturing her thoughtful blue gaze and holding it in brooding silence, Javier realised that he was in the grip of something seldom experienced: uncertainty.

Why was she looking thoughtful? Why hadn't she jumped at his offer? What was there to think about? They still wanted one another, neither of them was in this for the long haul and they had to let it run its course or risk it interfering with their working relationship when they returned to it.

And, from a more personal perspective, Javier could see that once they returned to London his hunt for a wife would become serious business. This was his window, probably his last window, of carefree sexual pleasure.

And, more than that, this was… He frowned and didn't follow that thought. Instead he focused on her thoughtful expression. Neither of them wanted complications and that was the main thing. So where was the problem?

It was an effort to sit in silence and wait for her to say something. Always in control of events, Javier was unsettled at the way he now felt out of his depth and controlled by something over which he had no say. He had a moment of wondering whether this was the right thing. It made sense on paper. He still wanted her so badly it was overwhelming, and yet…

He had this weird feeling of not being in control… Should he be wary of it? Had he somehow become vulnerable because his deadline was now set in stone? Vulnerable to the need to snatch fun while he still had the chance?

'Well?' he finally prompted in a voice that was a lot heartier than he was actually feeling.

'I think it's a good idea.'

Javier hadn't realised that he'd been stressed out waiting for her to respond until she actually responded, and then he half-smiled with relief and satisfaction.

'I'll have to sort stuff out with Benji.'

'If it's a problem, you can bring him over,' Javier said magnanimously.

'*Bring him over?* I didn't think you were that fond of dogs.'

'You'll miss him, and I have no problem with arranging transport for him.'

'A yacht might be a little much. I'm not sure how good a swimmer he is. Plus, there are loads of formalities involved when it comes to getting a dog from the UK into Europe.'

'You hardly have to worry about such things with me.' He clicked his finger and shot her a smile of utter satisfaction. He was the magician pulling rabbits out of the hat and impressing his audience. 'Put it this way, I wouldn't want you to spare a thought for shortening our time together because you're missing the dog. He's old and, trust me, there's sufficient room for him to stretch his legs, and we'll disembark on a regular basis. He can come with us and explore the wonders of the second-smallest country in the world.'

Their eyes tangled and Caitlin lowered her eyes as a thought flashed through her head.

Surely this was more than just sex for him? The fact that he was prepared to dump work, enjoy what they had and, furthermore, do what it took to make her day complete by getting Benji over—wasn't that above and beyond? He might laugh off what they had as just something physical that he had to get out of his system…but maybe he didn't see that there might just be something more lurking just beneath the surface.

'Okay.' She smiled and was flooded with warmth. 'I would love to see Monaco, and I'm pretty sure Benji would as well…'

CHAPTER NINE

MONACO WAS A SMALL, busy city on steroids. It reeked of wealth. This was where the rich came to play and frolic, and there was evidence of that everywhere—from the decadent casinos, where the stakes were high, to the eye-wateringly expensive designer malls and the opulent bars and clubs. Under glittering blue skies, beautiful people drifted by, carelessly swinging their designer totes and hiding behind oversized sunglasses.

The atmosphere was lazy and decadent and Javier told her a few facts about the place that made her eyes widen. One in three people living in the city, he'd said, were millionaires, and most of them were not natives of Monaco at all but there to take advantage of the generous tax breaks.

'Would *you* live here?' she'd asked on day one as they'd sat people-watching outside one of the smart cafés with a couple of ice-cold cocktails in front of them.

'I'd die of boredom!' He had laughed in response and his eyes had lingered when he'd added in a wicked undertone, 'Unless you were living here with me. The hot sex might make it worthwhile.'

The common-sense, down-to-earth part of Caitlin

knew that those were words thrown out there in the moment, meaning nothing, and yet she couldn't help herself from storing them up and reading into them feelings that might run deeper than he was prepared to admit.

So what if he and Isabella had embarked on a marriage of convenience? She had no idea why Isabella had called it off at the last minute; perhaps she had had cold feet at the thought of marrying for business and not love. She knew women could be sentimental in ways that men sometimes couldn't fathom.

And maybe, deep down, Javier himself had longed for something more than a contract to unite two powerful families with ties that went back for decades. He cared deeply for the woman, however he categorised it, and Caitlin felt that maybe, just maybe, he was capable of love...*wanted* love...even if that was something he would never voice in a million years.

Had she come into his life to find him in a place where he was actually ready to fall in love, even though he made so many noises about not believing in it? Caitlin knew that it was crazy to speculate but, with every passing second, she just knew she could see evidence of a guy who felt more for her than he was prepared to say out loud.

This was stolen time, but when that stolen time came to an end would he look at her and realise that she was indispensable? Realise that she had crept into his heart, the way he had crept into hers? Would he realise that arranged marriages that made sense were not what they were cracked up to be? Would he realise that he might talk the talk till he was blue in the face but he couldn't actually walk the walk now that he had invited her into his heart?

The fact that he'd brought Benji over said a lot. Caitlin had no idea what Tricia would be making of their prolonged absence but she knew that he remained on top of everything, waking before five to kill a load of emails. She, too, had fallen into a routine of catching up on stuff, working with him as she always had, but free to touch him because there were no curious eyes on his yacht.

Largely, they had a routine. Javier had managed to employ someone to take Benji out first thing for an hour and after that, while Benji snored his way through most of the day, they worked, talked, worked, made love, and had breakfast and lunch, sometimes in the nude, just for the hell of it.

The yacht was pretty amazing. It was not the biggest moored in the crystal-blue water, because there were a few far bigger ones bobbing here and there in the distance, but it was big enough, and kitted to the highest standard. There were three en suite bedrooms, staff quarters, an amazing kitchen and living quarters with pale leather seating. Two circular pools were perched on the upper deck, one with a Jacuzzi, and there was a fully stocked bar with bar-stools and tan leather seating against the sides, along with deck chairs and umbrellas.

And, in the bowels of the yacht, was lodged a six-seater black-and-red motor boat perfect for covering the distance between the yacht and the shore. Caitlin didn't know who was more impressed by the speedboat—Benji or her. They hopped on board, with Javier at the helm, and eyes closed, she enjoyed every second of the experience as they sped towards the city.

Right now, encased by a moonlit night, Caitlin was as relaxed as she could possibly be on one of the loungers by the pool with Benji in his bed next to her on the deck. She heard the rustle of Javier behind her, and turned lazily to watch as he shoved a deck chair close to hers and settled on it, handing her a glass of wine.

It was still very warm and he was in a pair of faded swimming trunks and a white linen shirt cuffed to the elbow, which was flapping open, affording her a fantastic view of his hard, brown torso with its sprinkling of dark hair. She was in her bikini bottoms, a new purchase from one of the boutiques in Monaco, and had discarded the top at some point in the evening, probably just before they'd made passionate love after dinner.

It was a struggle, resisting all his attempts to lavish her with *stuff*, but she remained savvy enough to know that accepting presents from him would do nothing for her self-respect when everything came crashing down. So she'd dug into her savings and added 'poverty' to the tally of all the things she would have to deal with when the inevitable happened.

It was worth it. Deep inside her, she knew that.

'Beautiful night…' she breathed, sitting up and shamelessly enjoying the sight of Javier.

'I'd forgotten how impressive the landscape here is,' he admitted, gazing out to sea, his arm lightly touching hers as he sipped the wine.

'Who uses this yacht when you're not on it?' Cait-

lin asked curiously, twisting a bit so that she was looking at him.

'Family members. Occasionally my father and his
cronies. Some of them enjoy time out from their better halves.'

'You've told me a bit about your family,' Caitlin
began. 'I know you were devastated when your mother
died. I would be as well in your shoes. I suppose I had
years of my mother failing to be a mother, so by the time
she died I had already grieved for her in some ways.
How did your mother die?'

'I'm thinking this isn't subject matter for a beautiful evening.'

'Guess not.'

Caitlin immediately backed off. He'd said so much
about himself but would he want to be reminded of it?

'Cancer,' he finally said heavily. 'It was quick. Not a
lot of time to say goodbye.'

'I'm so sorry…and you're right; this isn't the sort
of conversation to have when there's a bright moon in
the sky and we can hear the sound of the water lapping
against the side of the boat.'

'I was away at school at the time. I boarded from a
young age. Arrangements were made and, by the time
I returned, my mother was already dangerously close to
death. It was…shocking how gaunt she'd become. I think
she may well have known that something was wrong,
but she wasn't a complainer. She would have laughed
off the weight loss and the tiredness until she couldn't
any longer. At any rate, I was with her for a handful
of weeks, by which time she was too weak to engage.'

This was the most Javier had ever said to her about the details of his mother's death and Caitlin felt a bloom of tender satisfaction as yet another small window opened up, letting her inside.

'I know you said that your dad went off the rails a bit after she died because he couldn't cope with the loss...'

She wanted to pursue this conversation, even though she knew that she was treading a thin line, because if those shutters slammed harder then she might be shut out for good, but she was greedy to see more of him.

Javier shifted. She was prying but he'd already told her so much about himself and he couldn't understand how that had happened. Her questions were so lazy and gentle, and opened up a side to him in a way he couldn't quite get a grip on.

Did he want to have this conversation when touching her would have been more than plenty? It jarred, didn't it, sitting out here and talking about things he'd spent his adult life burying, yet again?

Yet, he was uncomfortably besieged by memories that filled his head like marauding wasps. He remembered how his father had cocooned himself and then emerged to have a catastrophic, short-lived fling with a gold-digger who had ended up conning him out of millions. The depth of his pain, hurt and bewilderment hit him with the force of a sledgehammer.

'Not the time or the place, Caitlin.'

'Understood.'

'What we have...here and now...isn't about this.'

The lines of what exactly they had in the here and now formed a blurry smudge in his head and he frowned.

'About what?'

'We've talked…we've had to, given the circumstances…but that doesn't mean that the talking has to continue. Caitlin, when we return to London, all this is forgotten. Personal conversations of this nature will have no place in a work environment.'

'Honestly, Javier, I didn't mean to barge past any "keep out" signs. I guess, growing up in foster care, I spent a lot of time imagining what life was like for other kids. Not that we didn't meet other kids, we did, but I always felt like an outsider.'

'A lonely life.' Javier felt the treacherous swirl of a current under his feet, dragging him back to the very place he had just closed off. 'But,' he said bracingly, 'loneliness can make a person strong.'

He was relieved when he heard the buzz of his mobile next to him. It gave him an excuse to stand up and head indoors, excusing himself while staring down at the phone.

Caitlin watched as he strode away into the bowels of the yacht. Every shared confidence fed the love inside her and watered the hope that wouldn't listen to common sense and go away.

Suddenly the void that had opened up at the thought of returning to London and handing in her resignation started to close. For the first time there was light at the end of a dark tunnel. First, he'd extended their time together. He'd wanted more than just sex, because if it had only been about sex, then he would never have confided in her, opened himself up. Yes, there had been times when she had caught some fleeting expression on his face that was soft and unguarded and had struck right to the core of her.

Then, he had personally arranged to have Benji flown over. That had been a giveaway because, as thoughtful and considerate as he was as a boss, getting Benji over had been well beyond the call of duty, and lust.

She idly stroked behind Benji's ear and relaxed back in the deck chair. She could hear very distant sounds coming from the shore and, looking across, the glittering lights were like stars studded against the shoreline. The air was balmy and carried the fragrance of the ocean, salty and fresh.

She wondered how she could broach the subject of trying to make this wonderful thing they had together work. How could he contemplate walking away from what they had so that he could embark on finding a woman who met a checklist but with whom he would probably have nothing in common?

Maybe if he hadn't confided in her… But he had, and he was a clever guy—clever enough to understand that, if he'd been affected by the past, it didn't mean all doors were closed. His head might say that, but she'd seen his heart, and his heart wouldn't agree.

Lost in swirling thoughts, but feeling ever more excited and hopeful with each passing moment, Caitlin was barely aware of Javier padding back across the deck until he subsided onto the lounger. When he looked at her there was a smile of satisfaction on his face. With only subdued lighting on the upper deck and the radiance of the moon, his beautiful face was all shadows and angles and thrillingly sexy.

'Good phone call?' Caitlin smiled and reached out to cover his hand with hers, moving to link their fingers, and for once not hiding the tenderness in her eyes.

'Excellent phone call. Isabella.'

'Really?'

'There's something you need to know, Caitlin.'

'What's that?' Her voice was wary and, as their eyes met, he smiled.

'Nothing for you to worry about, no need to look as though I'm about to tell you that the sky is falling down. It's about Isabella… There are certain things I omitted from the story, certain facts that… Okay, how shall I put it…were not within my remit to tell you, but I can tell you now because they've finally and terrifically been made public.'

'I'm intrigued.' She liked the sound of 'nothing for her to worry about'.

'As you know, for both myself and Isabella, our marriage was something that made sense and suited us both equally.'

'A marriage of convenience. Literally a business partnership.'

'Beyond the business practicalities, it suited us emotionally. Friends but not lovers, and so no emotional complications.'

'I'm still intrigued.'

'It suited Isabella because she's gay.'

Silence stretched between them, and Caitlin knew

that her mouth had dropped open because this was the last thing she'd been expecting.

'As in…'

'As in the normal definition of the word,' Javier said wryly. 'She's had a partner for nearly three years and I've always known about her preferences. I was probably one of the first and the few she shared that intimate secret with, and I've obviously been duty-bound to keep it to myself, hence I've said nothing to you earlier.'

He was smiling now and looking into the distance. 'I've encouraged her over the years to come clean but she's been scared stiff at how her father might react and, when his health began deteriorating, even more apprehensive. There was also the matter of an extremely traditional board of directors who would have had to accept something they might have found a little unexpected, although I personally thought that she was over-apprehensive on that count. Time's moved on since the bad old days. But, largely, it was her father's possible reaction that pushed her into accepting our marriage of convenience.'

'What happened to change that?'

'Her girlfriend gave her an ultimatum, and Isabella took a deep breath and did what she knew she should have done a long time ago—she told her father who, incidentally, is recovering extremely well and is already itching to get back to work.

'By the way, she sends her love and apologises profusely if you thought that she was messing you around. When she disappeared without warning on that wedding dress viewing day, it was because her girlfriend had run out of patience and contacted her to return to Spain to sort things out or else she wouldn't be there waiting in the shadows.'

'Wow.'

'You're shocked?'

'Surprised at you choosing to marry Isabella under those circumstances. That…that must have been a sacrifice for you, Javier. I know family bonds mean a lot, but still…'

'Oh, the marriage also suited me, quite aside from the family bonds, strong as those were.'

'How so?'

'Long story, Caitlin…' He hesitated but only momentarily. 'I inherit vineyards in Spain when I turn thirty-five, but only if I marry.' He grimaced. 'Getting hold of those vineyards means a great deal to me. Isabella would have been the perfect solution. As it stands, I have to find another suitable wife, and my timeline isn't exactly generous.'

'Another suitable wife…'

'Well, my parameters for marrying still stand, and now there's a sense of urgency to my search because time isn't going to stand still and wait for me to catch up.'

Caitlin stared. What a fool she had been. There was no door opening in his heart. What planet had she been on? He still wanted, and would only ever want, the sort of woman who would never make demands on him. Isabella would have been perfect, but in her absence he would find a suitably high-born Spanish woman who knew the rules of the game and would be content to be mistress of his empire without demanding love and attention.

Without demanding heart-to-heart chats…and giggling and laughter. And maybe just having sex to make babies, although clearly even that wasn't a prerequisite. He and Isabella would presumably have left the baby-making part to the doctors.

The simmering euphoria she had felt just moments before, when she had been so convinced that what Javier felt was more than just lust, evaporated like dew on a hot summer's morning. He'd told her that he wasn't into commitment, that what he wanted would always be a manufactured business arrangement without the complications of emotion. Instead of listening, she had eventually chosen to play with the fantasy that he didn't know himself as well as she knew him.

She had interpreted his behaviour and jumped to conclusions, but the hard truth was that all he wanted from her was the hot sex. He might have confided in her, they might have laughed together and she might have built her castles in the air based on those things, but Javier lived in a black-and-white world and love was never going to intrude. He was never going to be open to persuasion.

'You've gone quiet on me.'

Caitlin blinked and focused. 'It was very brave of Isabella to face up to her sexuality and tell her dad. It couldn't have been easy. I can understand why you're proud of her, because you care about her.'

'Why am I getting the feeling that something's going on under the surface here?'

Caitlin took a deep breath and grappled with a way forward. 'I guess I'm a diehard romantic after all,' she said quietly. 'I never thought your marriage was *that* much of a cold business arrangement.'

'Far from cold.'

'For you to be prepared to face a future without... without...a future without any semblance of... Where you'd be both living separate romantic lives...'

'Where are you going with this, Caitlin?'

'And then,' she murmured, 'to hear that the deal suited you because you want to inherit some vineyards when you already have wealth beyond imagining... And to hear you say that you're now time-pressured to find a candidate to fill the role of your wife—someone who doesn't expect anything other than to run your households while you go about your business having fun on the side, because fun on the side would never involve any emotional involvement...'

'Tell me what's going on here. I thought I was being honest with you.'

'You are. I just thought...'

'That somewhere along the line I was going to fall in love with Isabella and live happily ever after? Even though I told you that love and everything that goes with it wasn't for me?' He tilted his head to one side and looked at her narrowly.

Caitlin saw it. She saw the light bulb going off in his head as he joined the dots and worked out what was going on with her. The silence gathered around them as they stared at one another and Javier hissed a sigh and raked his fingers through his hair.

'Caitlin…'

'So, I was a fool.' She snatched the top she had earlier discarded and shoved it on.

'I thought I'd made it clear…'

'You did. Like I said, I was an idiot. I… I never thought in a million years that we would ever end up sleeping together, Javier.' She was as tense as a bowstring. What happens next? she wondered.

She hadn't originally planned to pour out her heart, but then again she hadn't expected to be confronted with information that challenged everything she'd clung to. She gritted her teeth and stuck her chin out at a defiant angle.

'But,' she said tightly, 'we did and, yes, you did warn me off, but I just didn't have the good sense to protect my heart.' She lowered her eyes because she didn't want to see his expression: appalled horror; mouth slack with dismay; frantic glances towards the nearest escape route…

'No,' she said with wrenching honesty. 'Maybe I didn't want to protect my heart or, if I did, I wanted you more for whatever little time we had together.'

'This is a conversation we shouldn't be having, *querida*.'

'Why not? And *don't* call me *querida*! *Querida* is the last thing I am to you!'

'Caitlin, let's not go there!'

'Why not? Because it's a scary place? Where's the point in not being honest with yourself?'

'I can think of a thousand reasons off the top of my head.'

'When we were together, Javier, I felt I saw something in you, *sensed* something in you—something that made me think that there was more between us than you're probably willing to admit.'

'I don't do emotion.'

'I have no idea what that means. You've never explained exactly what that means! How can someone not *do emotion*? You're not a robot!'

'Let's drop this.'

'It's time for me to hand in my resignation, Javier.'

Like an unstoppable train gathering momentum, there was no way she could stop now, and she didn't want to. She'd always planned to enjoy what she could of the guy she loved before walking away with her pride intact, but then the minute she had seen chinks in his armour everything had changed. She'd started to entertain the thought that she could change him. She'd started to believe that he would be able to see what they had as something deserving of a shot, as something more than just the fling he'd told her it was.

Surely no one was *immune* to emotion, the way he said he was? But he'd been prepared to marry Isabella and live a life devoid of any chance of real love. He was now prepared to marry some unknown, suitable woman and happily live his life in an emotional vacuum. Because he'd really meant what he'd told her about wanting a particular sort of woman—a woman who made sense, with no hearts and flowers attached to the relationship.

'Clearly, I was foolish. I thought you'd just never fallen in love with anyone before but that maybe, just maybe, what we had had changed that. When you offered to bring Benji over, I jumped to the conclusion that you must feel more than just lust, because you really wanted to do something you knew would make me happy. I couldn't have been more mistaken!'

It was cleansing, having her say after all this time bottling up what she felt. She could feel the weight lifting off her shoulders and realised that somewhere deep inside, when she got past the 'living in the moment' philosophy, she'd been terrifyingly aware of the day of reckoning lurking round the corner.

'It's a bit difficult to storm off when you're sitting on a yacht in the middle of the ocean, but I'll leave as soon as humanly possible.' Her voice was flat and hard.

Javier felt as though he'd just been hit with a sledgehammer when he'd least been expecting it. He'd been pleased with Isabella's news. She'd faced down her demons; every fear she'd had had proven unfounded and she'd been over the moon. He hadn't thought twice about sharing the news with Caitlin. Left to him, he would have told her from the very start, but of course it hadn't been his story to tell.

Now, when he reflected grimly, he could see that he hadn't been thinking *at all* when it came to Caitlin. He'd made a few perfunctory remarks, laying down his ground rules, but he'd been so busy enjoying himself, enjoying *her*, that he'd taken his eye off the ball big time.

He cast his mind back now to the way he'd dropped his guard, and paled, because it was almost as though he'd learnt nothing from the past. He'd lived in a ridiculous, manufactured bubble and forgotten all the principles of self-control he'd always lived by. He hadn't been himself, and he couldn't understand *why*, but the one thing he *did* understand was that she'd mistakenly read all sorts of things into his behaviour and he couldn't blame her.

He was man enough to accept the blame for the mess in which he now found himself. He'd drifted and, if he could pinpoint a moment when that drift had started, it was when he had seen her in her full glory twirling on a stool in a wedding dress for a wedding that wasn't to be. The sight had knocked him for six and had lodged in his head like a burr, like something waiting to be released the minute the opportunity came along, and along had come that opportunity when the wedding had been called off.

And since then he'd ignored all alarm bells and red flags. He'd played truant from work for the first time in his life. He'd opened up about himself in ways he couldn't remember doing. *Was it any wonder that she had begun to feel all sorts of things about a relationship that had been a lot more casual for him?*

He thought back to the flash of consternation he had felt when he'd found out that she was a virgin, and the ease with which he had dismissed any concern that she might have been a lot more vulnerable emotionally than she'd stoutly announced. She'd implied that he wasn't her type, and he'd decided to go along with that, and not once had he bothered to reflect on whether that continued to hold true once they'd become truly intimate.

'Caitlin...' He raked his fingers through his hair and shifted.

'You don't have to say anything.'

'You made it clear that I wasn't the sort of guy you were looking for.' To his own ears, the protest sounded pathetic.

'You still aren't, but I've found out that hearts don't always play by the rules. I'm going to head in now.' She stood up and backed away from him. 'I'll get my things from your room and pack. I'll need to know about arrangements for returning to London.'

'I would say that I don't want you to resign but…'

'I was going to before I told you how I felt. I was going to walk away because it would have been impossible for me to carry on working for you.'

'You would have left me in the *lurch*?'

'Yes.'

'If I could promise you what you want…'

'I wouldn't believe you anyway,' Caitlin told him sharply. 'I know how the cards stack up now. Good luck finding whatever it is you're looking for so that you can get your vineyards.'

'I can arrange everything for tomorrow. No need for you to wait for a flight; my man will take you in my private jet. If you'd rather, I can even arrange an overnight stay in a hotel on the mainland should you find our arrangement here…er…somewhat uncomfortable.'

In a flash, Caitlin knew with biting bitterness where Javier was going with this. She'd outlived her usefulness by confessing that she loved him. That wasn't part of the game and never had been. Now he wanted her out as fast as possible. That hurt—really hurt.

'Good idea,' she said tightly. 'How long do I have?'

'I'm not rushing you off my yacht...'

'Of course you are,' Caitlin snapped dismissively, scooping up Benji and burrowing against him as she stared at Javier with simmering, edgy hostility. She lowered her eyes and gathered herself because he hadn't asked for this, and just because he wanted to get rid of her now didn't make him a monster. He just couldn't return her love and was dealing with what she had thrown at him the best he could.

She turned away to feel his hand circling her arm, tugging her gently back until she wanted to pass out from the nearness of him.

'Caitlin.' His voice was ragged, barely audible. 'You don't have to do this...'

'Do what?'

'Go. You don't have to go. We can pretend this conversation never happened.'

'Of course we can't,' she said flatly. 'And I wouldn't want to.' But there was a flare of triumph inside her because she knew then that, even if he didn't love her, he really, really *wanted* her. Maybe she wouldn't fade from his head as fast as all the others who had preceded her. It was scant comfort, but it was some.

She tugged her arm free and backed away, still looking at him, while Benji threatened to let the side down by leaping out of her arms and making a fool of himself by wanting to play with the guy staring at her.

Javier broke the silence. 'I'll arrange a hotel. And someone to take you to the mainland in the speedboat. Won't be longer than an hour at most.' He flushed darkly.

'Perfect.' Caitlin smiled tersely. 'And then you can move on with your life, Javier, and thank your lucky stars that you successfully dodged a bullet.'

'And you?'

'Believe it or not, when you've lived the life that I have, you can overcome anything.'

What a lie, but she left him with that thought as she spun round on her heels and walked away.

CHAPTER TEN

JAVIER STARED OUT of the window of his vast office down to a crowded London street several storeys beneath him. The office was empty. Why wouldn't it be? It was Saturday, it was a little past five on a sunny afternoon and most people with anything resembling a life were out there enjoying what passed for the great outdoors in London. The parks would be crammed, the cafés would be heaving, the pavements spilling over with crowds drinking and enjoying the ongoing fine weather.

He missed her. For a few days after she'd left, he'd gone back over what she had told him and had picked apart every word spoken, every admission of how she felt, every valiant declaration of love. Then, for a few more days, he'd told himself that she'd been spot on when she'd said that he'd dodged a bullet because the last thing he wanted was the sort of love and romance that was always riddled with complication and disappointment.

Javier grimaced now as he thought back to the optimistic dates he had set in motion—potential candidates. They'd been easy to source, because he knew almost everyone who belonged to the elite social set in which he'd always mixed in Spain. He'd had one conversation with Isabella and the rest had been a matter of the grapevine. It didn't matter about the marriage that had never been. All that mattered was that the most eligible guy in Europe was single and ready to settle down.

He'd been on one date and had backed off after an hour of surreptitious watch-looking and thoughts of Caitlin that wouldn't leave his head. He'd told himself that he just needed a bit more time. He knew what was good for him, knew that love was not something he wanted, or indeed was even capable of subscribing to. It was good that she was no longer in his life because that inevitably would have led to demands for things he couldn't give her.

What was the point of lessons learnt if they got thrown down the drain just because he got caught on the back foot? He wasn't built for love and that was the end of it. So it wasn't a case of any genie let out of any bottle, no wayward emotion that accounted for his restless nights and lack of concentration at work. It was just that he needed a bit more time.

But how he remembered the way she smiled...the way she laughed...the way her blue eyes had lingered on him...the flush in her cheeks after they'd made love and the way she could touch him so that in seconds his body went up in flames.

And he also remembered stuff he maybe wanted to forget: the way he'd felt comfortable talking to her; the way they'd lain in bed in the warm afterglow of good sex and he'd talked to her about anything and everything.

He'd intellectually accepted the sort of woman he

would need to replace Isabella—the wife who understood everything he had to offer and accepted it. It was the same mental picture he'd planted in his head from a young age, when he'd understood the dangers of loving too much, loving so much that it made a person weak instead of strong. She would be wealthy in her own right, able to manage the life he led without need for guidance, because his work life would have to remain uninterrupted. She would be happy to enjoy the fruits of his vast fortune without nagging for attention, clinging or needing validation. She would be as emotionally independent as he was. The last thing she would want was *romance*.

But, rubbing alongside that mental image was the reality of a woman who was the complete opposite to that. A woman who wanted and needed love and devotion. A woman who hugged, cuddled and snuggled, and did all the things he'd always made sure to discourage in past relationships.

And even before they'd become lovers...

She was a woman who grounded him and could tease him out of his stress. He'd accepted it all as part and parcel of her proficiency at her job but it had been a whole lot more than that. While he'd been busy thinking about the boundaries he'd set down, supposedly never to be breached, he'd failed to realise that she'd spent the weeks, months and years slowly breaching every one of them in small, incremental steps.

He thought of the times when she'd worked late, when they'd shared a takeaway and she'd somehow managed to convince him not to do an all-nighter. Thought of the anecdotes about Benji, the softness in her voice when she'd talked about him, the way that softness had pierced into the heart of him and lodged there.

And then later, when he'd found out about her childhood…everything had come together. The warmth had flooded him then; he'd felt tenderness. Realisation came slowly because he fought it tooth and nail. He didn't want to admit, even to himself, that love had crept up on him, ambushing all the self-control he had thought would always protect him.

But all those dots being joined up would not allow him the luxury of pretending that he felt nothing for her. What he felt was the despair of denying the love that had blossomed inside him, eating up all his objections and turning him into the kind of guy who closed his laptop and stopped caring when he next opened it.

Javier stared down blindly at the busy roads below and felt a sickening churning in his stomach, the pain of turning his back on something he should have grabbed with both hands.

What the hell happened now? That was what he was thinking. How did he approach the situation? Did he leave it? Climb back into his ivory tower and tell himself that it was for the best?

Nearly a month had gone by! She'd said her piece and disappeared off the face of the earth. He hadn't even had a company contact him for a reference. Was she looking for another job? Was she still living in London, come to it?

Had she turned her back on him for ever?

He had her mobile number, and he knew that he could

simply call, but he hadn't...*had he*? He'd lost count of the number of times over the passing weeks when he'd looked at that number in his phone and backed away from calling it while he'd stupidly carried on the pretence that he was still in charge of his emotions.

For the first time in his life, Javier was scared: scared of opening up to her about how he felt; scared of *not* opening up to her about how he felt; scared of emotions that were so big he barely knew how to handle them or what to do with them; scared at the thought of a future without her in it.

And, most of all, scared of making a move only for her to turn her back and walk away from him as he sickeningly suspected she would. She'd laid her cards on the table, and so had he, and he doubted she would want anything to do with him, having been firmly knocked back and shown the door.

He had never been a guy to succumb to creating scenarios in his head but Javier now found that creating scenarios in his head was just about the only thing he seemed capable of doing. He had no idea how to approach her and he knew that, with every passing day, the chances of her listening to a word he had to say became more and more remote.

Fed up with the state of indecision which had been his state of mind for weeks, Javier swung round, picked up his mobile and began scrolling through it while walking to the door.

It felt good to take charge of the situation and, in the end, what would be would be...

* * *

Caitlin hit Kensington Gardens at pace because she'd been held up every step of the way, and it had sounded urgent when Angie had made the arrangement for them to meet. Which, frankly, wasn't like her friend at all. She was the most laid-back person on the face of the earth. So, when she had called the day before and asked her in a hurry whether they could meet at a designated spot in the park at a designated time, and that *it was important*, Caitlin had been instantly concerned. She'd asked questions, but in the background she could hear dogs barking, so she hadn't been surprised that few of her questions were answered because Angie was in a rush.

Anyway, she'd been glad that the conversation had been brief. There'd been no time for Angie to pry into how her time out had gone because Caitlin wasn't sure how good she would be at pretending it was all fine and dandy in the world.

It wasn't. The past few weeks had been hell. Like an addict with the supply of the love drug she had overdosed on severed without warning, the withdrawal was agony; no other word for it. She hadn't even been able to get her act together to start job hunting. She was relying on her savings to get her through the temporary apathy which was all-consuming.

It made her desperately sad to think that this was the sort of time when a daughter might flee back to her mum, but in the absence of any family all she could do was try and fix herself with no shoulder to cry on.

She tried to remember every passing expression that

had crossed Javier's face when she had blurted out how she felt about him. When her memory refused to play along, she became adept at filling in the gaps herself: horror; dismay; probably revulsion, which he had hidden well, because he would have been conscious not to hurt her feelings. Still, he had swept her out of his life like some debris he'd needed to clear asap, and that hurt, however much she tried to rationalise it.

Had she made a mistake in pouring out her heart? That had not been the original intention but, the minute she had got it into her head that his feelings for her ran deeper than he thought, she had thrown caution to the winds and started building all sorts of stupid fairy-tale castles in her head. She had been so blinded by her own love, and so heady at the thought that what they had was the real thing, that she had conveniently forgotten everything he had said about the sort of person he wanted in his life until that call from Isabella had come through. That person was not her. He had to marry, but never to a woman like her, because his emotions she'd thought she'd tapped into had been a mirage.

She hadn't heard a peep out of him since leaving his yacht and that hurt. Yet why would he contact her? What would he say? That he was sorry she'd misread the situation, and *have a good life*?

She sprinted from the bus across the busy road, tugging Benji, who was looking around him with ears cocked, tail wagging, tongue lolling and a sprint in his ageing step. The change of scenery had got him going and he was looking madly around as she stooped to let him off the lead. He would follow her; he always did.

At five in the afternoon, it was still hot and the place was packed. And she was late, by ten minutes. She kept looking around as she headed to their meeting place, making sure Benji didn't decide to start exploring their new, exciting environment.

She knew exactly where to go because she and her friend had met many times in the same spot over the years, Angie for her dog walking, and she with Benji, because the company was great. But when she peered through the crowds, there was no sign of Angie, and she frowned, tapping into the message on her phone to make sure she'd got the place right, when she heard someone calling from behind her.

They were calling for Benji. And it wasn't Angie's voice. In fact, it took a couple of seconds for Caitlin even to realise that it was a man's voice, and even longer for her to realise who the man in question was.

She turned around slowly. Shock made her numb. She could barely breathe and her thoughts clouded over as she balanced a fine line between disbelief and dawning realisation.

Javier. After no word from him for weeks—radio silence. She'd poured out her heart to him and, not only had he politely sent her on her way, but he hadn't seen fit to send so much as a text to ask her whether she was okay. It was obvious that he hadn't given a jot about her in the end. He'd cared *a lot* about the sex, and he'd been affectionate enough when they'd been together, but that affection had been generated by the physical relationship they'd shared and, when the physicality had ended, so had the affection.

She felt the colour mount in her cheeks as she looked at Javier in the distance, her treacherous dog bounding towards him like a long-lost pal. He wasn't walking towards her and he was dangling...*were those sausages?*... to tempt Benji, who would have needed next to no temptation, because he had developed a shameful attachment to her ex-boss.

Caitlin felt the shock and disbelief coalesce into white-hot rage. How dared he, after all this time, seek her out via her *lily-livered dog*? How dared he *just show up* without warning? How dared he ambush her when she was still fragile and hurting and desperate to forget all about him?

Yet, on one very important level, she was aware of that dark current of excitement underneath her anger, an excitement that had continued to simmer, unabated, all through her sadness and disillusionment. Which only made her more furious.

As she looked, he dangled a sausage before tossing it to Benji. His eyes were fastened on her. God, it was unfair how drop-dead gorgeous he still looked. Couldn't he have gone downhill in the interim—stacked on some weight, lost all his hair? Could he have done anything, become *anything*, that could no longer hurt her the way he was hurting her right now?

Why was he here? That was the question that raged inside her as she remained glued to the spot for a few seconds. Had he come to try and get her back into bed? Or maybe her replacement wasn't living up to expectation and he actually thought that, with some time now between them, he could woo her back into her old job and they could both pretend that nothing had happened between them. Either way, she was going to put him straight on both counts!

That would mean walking over there on her leaden feet. Benji was showing no sign of returning to base camp. He was zooming around Javier with crazy fervour and Caitlin lacked the nerve to yell for him to come back, mostly knowing that there was a good chance she would be ignored. Besides, people would stare. A lot of people were already surreptitiously staring at Javier. He had that effect on other people, male and female alike.

Caitlin propelled herself forward and, the closer she got to where Javier was reaching into a bag to produce another treat, the more her heartbeat quickened. Seeing him again was like seeing him for the first time—the time when she had walked into his office for the interview that would change her life and had forgotten how to breathe because she'd never seen anyone so beautiful.

'What are you doing here?' were her opening words as she pulled to a stop in front of him and glared, first at him and then at Benji. 'How did you know where I would be?'

'I phoned your doggy friend.'

'She had no right to tell you!'

'It's a public place, and besides—'

'Besides *what*? And stop giving Benji those sausages! He's not allowed them! Did you purposefully come here armed with treats for my dog because you knew he wouldn't be able to resist? That I would have to come over here and talk to you? Because I don't want to talk to you, Javier. I've done enough talking to you to last a lifetime!'

Caitlin looked away quickly because she could feel tears begin to prick the back of her eyes. She stooped, reached for Benji's collar and began putting his lead back on. She was only aware of Javier stooping to her level when she felt his shadow on her and the warmth of his body so close to hers that she could have reached out and stroked his beautiful face with no effort at all.

She looked up and her blue, glassy eyes collided with deep, dark ones; she felt a jolt of agonising awareness.

'I was afraid that, if I called you, you would refuse to see me,' Javier murmured in a low, shaky voice. 'And, Caitlin, I needed to see you.'

'I'm not falling back into bed with you, Javier, and I'm not returning to work for you as though nothing's happened because you miss my skill set. I said that when I walked away weeks ago, and nothing's changed since then.'

She forced herself to stand, to break the electric connection between them. He remained where he was, stooping at her feet and idly rubbing behind Benji's ear, who dug in his canine heels when she tugged the lead.

Javier, playing with Benji, could feel her hostile eyes on him and he couldn't blame her. She hadn't asked to see him and, now that he had shown up, she wanted him gone.

Would it have been easier if he hadn't been such a blind fool for so long? If he had tried to see her sooner? Was it possible even to begin to fill the hole left behind in those weeks of stubborn silence on his part? And how could he begin to explain to her that, when he'd lived a lifetime being rigid, it had become the only thing he knew?

She'd fallen in love with him, but love could turn to hostile resentment at the flick of a switch, and he had deliberately flicked that switch weeks ago when he had scurried away from her declarations faster than a rat leaving a sinking ship. How could he begin to explain just how much things had changed for him? He could barely look at her.

'Tell your mistress,' he half-whispered unsteadily to Benji, who was panting in anticipation of something more exciting than conversations, 'that I love her.'

He remained where he was but raised his head to look at her.

Caitlin drew in a sharp breath. What could she read in those dark, fathomless eyes? She was scared to trust her instinct, which had spectacularly let her down before, but she had stopped tugging at Benji's lead and she found it hard to tear her eyes away from Javier. He said something to Benji in such a low voice that it was a strain to hear, and whatever he'd whispered was gluing her to the spot.

'What did you just say?' she asked tightly. Her blue eyes were narrowed and suspicious as he slowly stood up so that now he was gazing down at her, his handsome face darkly flushed. 'Because I'm done with you feeding Benji sausages.'

'I said that I love you.'

Caitlin loosed a laugh of pure disbelief. In the space of a few weeks, he'd gone from the guy who'd been relieved to see her walk away to the guy who suddenly *loved* her?

'And pigs fly,' she shot back. 'I don't need this. I don't want to talk to you!'

She spun round and, damn it, tears pricked the back of her eyes again. She yanked at Benji and began striding off, half-dragging the stubborn, resistant dog, knowing that Javier was following her and not quite sure how to deal with that.

Why was her reluctant heart yearning to hear what he had to say? Was she a glutton for punishment?

'Please, my darling, please let me talk. I'm begging you…'

'Don't!'

She stopped dead in her tracks.

'There's a tree over there. Let's go sit under it for five minutes. Let me say what I have to say and then, if you tell me to go, I'll walk away and you'll never be bothered by me again.'

Of course she was going to walk away! She refused to let her heart get the better of her head this time…

'Five minutes, then,' she said warily, turning round and walking at speed to the shady tree, while her heart picked up pace and her pulses began to race. She sat down and tried to focus on Benji while Javier sat at a respectable distance.

When she reluctantly and finally looked at him, her heart constricted, because he looked miserable and uncertain, and those were two things she had never seen in his repertoire before.

'I let you go,' Javier said hoarsely. 'And I should never have done that.'

'Because you miss the sex?' Caitlin mocked, but her heart was doing it again—beating like a sledgehammer and sending stupid thoughts racing through her head.

'Because I love you, *querida*.'

'You don't love me,' she said fiercely. 'And I told you *not* to call me that!'

'I understand why you might not want to believe me…'

'I poured my heart out to you and you were nothing but embarrassed for me—and then you got me the first ride back to London—so no, I don't believe a word you say.'

'Caitlin…'

'Are you going to deny that?'

'Like I said, I was an idiot. I… I didn't believe in love. That was something meant for other people, fools who got taken in by fairy tales only to wind up disenchanted and a hell of a lot poorer. My father rushed into a relationship that cost him dear. He wasn't there for me when I needed him because he got lost in his own grief, his own uncontrollable emotions. He never saw a son who was hurting. I vowed I would never let my emotions blind me. Duty and eventually a marriage of convenience was what was in store for me, and I liked the predictability of something that made sense.'

He raked his fingers through his hair.

'Marrying Isabella made sense. It killed two birds

with one stone. It sorted out her dilemma and it gave me the wife I needed to get the vineyards I wanted—which by the way I wanted because they hold happy memories of my childhood with my mother. I know it sounds ruthless that I was pursuing an inheritance but…most people aren't like you. Your childhood experiences… Somehow they didn't make you hard, bitter, I don't even know how—'

'If I could have had that protective covering,' Caitlin snapped through gritted teeth, 'do you think I would have ended up where I did?'

'I like where you ended up. I like where *we* ended up. I like the softness inside you, the honesty, the lack of guile. I think I always did. I just never acknowledged it.'

'Don't you *dare* say anything you don't mean,' Caitlin warned shakily, and Javier reached daringly to stroke her cheek, encouraged when she didn't push his hand away.

'I'm not. Everything I'm telling you is coming straight from my heart. From the start, you appealed to me in ways I never consciously registered. When Isabella broke off the relationship, it wasn't my intention to sleep with you but, looking back now, it feels as though fate had finally decided that I need to wake up and start seeing what it felt like to jump into the thing called life.'

'Fate came for me long before,' Caitlin haltingly responded. 'I always had a crush on you and it just didn't go away, even when Isabella came on the scene. I kept thinking that you getting married would open my eyes up to how stupid I was, but I still couldn't look at you without my whole body going up in flames.'

'I wish I'd known…'

'Why?'

'Because we might have started this thing between us, this amazing, wonderful thing, long ago—and maybe I wouldn't have wasted my time with women who came and went, in a mindset where the only relationship that seemed feasible was one that made sense. Nothing makes sense about the way I feel about you, *mi corazón*, and I never knew just how much I like it that way. When we were together…I forgot everything.'

'Even work.'

'Especially work. All I wanted was to be with you. I kidded myself that it was all about the mind-blowing sex, but there were times, so many times, when I looked at you and in my gut I knew that there was so much more to what I was feeling than lust.'

Every ounce of hesitation in Caitlin vanished at the utter sincerity in Javier's eyes and she reached forward and leaned into him. The cool feel of his mouth against hers ignited an explosion inside her that went straight from her head to between her thighs, and she sighed into his mouth before pulling back to trace the outline of his lips.

'It's what made me say what I did,' she confessed, hand flat against his chest. She stared past him thoughtfully. 'I thought that common sense would protect me from you, but I was wrong, and I realised that pretty quickly after we became lovers. And then… I sensed more than just lust. Maybe I was picking up some of the vibes you didn't know you were giving off, but the minute you offered to bring Benji over... Well, my imagination went into overdrive.'

'You came out with everything you felt.'

'It was a very comprehensive confession.' Caitlin grimaced.

'And my knee-jerk reaction was to run away.' He sighed and, when he kissed her, it was slowly and tenderly and their noses touched when he next spoke, voice low and quiet. 'But over the past few weeks I began to read all the writing that had been on the wall for so long, began to realise just how much I'd fallen in love with you and just what a fool I'd been to deny what was in my heart. I had no idea how I was going to get up the courage to come and see you, but then I figured that Benji might work as my intermediary.'

'He seems to have been a cheap trick when it comes to sharing his allegiances!' Caitlin laughed.

'So what I want to say...' Javier pulled back and looked at her gravely.

'What you want to say is...?'

'Will you marry me?'

Caitlin felt the damned tears again but this time tears of joy. There was no holding her back this time. She flung her arms around his neck, buried her face into him and whispered against him,

'Yes! Yes, yes, yes! My darling, wonderful Javier, for ever...'

* * * * *

   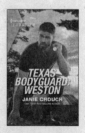